Copyright:

A Game of Inches

By: M. Nathaniel Gampel

Published by:

Simpel and Associates, LLC
136 Lexington Ave.
Edison, NJ 08817

www.simpelandassociates.com

For permissions contact:
Nathan Gampel at
info@simpelandassociates.com

Disclaimer:

This is a work of fiction. Names, characters, businesses, places, events, locales, and incidents are either the products of the author's imagination or used in a fictitious manner. Any resemblance to actual persons, living or dead, or actual events is purely coincidental.

Acknowledgements

2-years.

What a difference such a short sounding amount of time can mean to a life.

I set out to write Kinetic Transformation not because I expected to be a best seller or anything like that.

I wrote it because…

I simply had a question that never seemed to get answered.

And despite everyone telling me it was all good, I just couldn't believe it.

This unrelenting obsession with understanding the "general relativity" of change, known in the business world as "Transformation", has become both my personal and professional passions. And believe me when I say, I am grateful for the adventure every day.

Indeed, the Transformation Trilogy marks a milestone in my career and represents my contribution to the Transformation Sciences community at large. I am grateful for the opportunity to share my work and hope it provides a little education, insight, and fun in your everyday work life.

If this acknowledgement sounds a bit fantastic, well…it is. What my life has become since Book 1 could not have been imagined. And I am watching with bated breath, fear, and excitement to see where it all leads.

But whatever comes, one thing has not changed: my love and adoration for my family.

Everything begins with my one and only, Sara, to whom all my works are eternally dedicated. She is the real hero here. My hero. And I love her always.

To my children, who each make me proud and inspire me daily: you each bring something special and I am proud to be your father. Keep doing it and making us proud.

My father: the force of nature who still takes my calls, listens to my crazy ideas, and always has a yell at the ready. Thanks for eternally remaining "Machette." You help me to stop talking and start doing.

And of course, to our clients, employees, friends, and extended family. Nothing works without your support. I thank you every day for the opportunity you give me to live my dream as

Nathan Transformation.

Contents

Adversity: a Game of Inches

Once upon a time, a young friend of mine and his buddies were out doing what teenagers do – stuff they shouldn't be doing. We don't need a lot of details – let's just say there was "impaired judgment."

When the glass bottle shattered against the windshield, the guys thought it was hysterical – until they were surrounded by the flashing blue lights of the local constabulary.

The boys assumed "the position" on the hood of the squad car. During the pat down, one of the officers felt a suspicious-feeling lump in our protagonist's hip jeans pocket.

"What's this, son," he asked in his best Sgt. Friday[1] voice. "You got a weapon? Drugs?"

In one of those moments of teen inspiration, the detainee said (doing what he thought was a great Cosmo Kramer impersonation[2]), "Why, they're

---

[1] Joe Friday, played with gruff, predictable brilliance by Jack Webb on Dragnet (1952-1959, then – in a better-known version – 1967-1970 where Webb teamed up with Harry Morgan, who later portrayed Colonel Sherman Potter on M.A.S.H.).

[2] From "The Junior Mint" episode of Seinfeld, Season 4, Episode 20.

peppermints, Officer, and they're delicious. Ya gotta have one!"

For reasons unknown to this day, instead of putting the young men "into the system," the officer laughed, read the boys the riot act, and sent them home.

In *Any Given Sunday*[3], Al Pacino (playing aging football coach Tony D'Amato) is faced with a team that no longer respects him.

Or each other.

Somehow, the team has found itself in a playoff game against a team that in any normal universe should clobber them. The die is cast under a shroud of dark emotions, and it seems the outcome is predetermined.

In a final effort to repair the damage of the season and give his squad a fighting chance, Coach D'Amato decides to do something different.

Something all great leaders seem to do.

He asked for help.

> *"You know, when you get old in life, things get taken from you... That's part of life. But you only learn that*

---

[3] Warner Brothers, 1999. Oliver Stone, director.

when you start losing stuff. You find out life's a game of inches[4]."

"A game of inches" – that's what my young friend and his buddies encountered. Any shift in any part of the story – more damage to property – a snarky remark from one of the miscreants – an investigating officer who'd gotten cold eggs for breakfast – could have sent their lives spiraling in an entirely different direction.

Would they have become career criminals? Bond villains[5]? Probably not. But an arrest on a serious charge (and I left part of the story out to protect identities and such), and their future plans would have veered off course – at the very least.

Not everyone is as lucky. Some people don't get a break. Others do something so egregious that they deserve "time out" from society. This unending, sad reality of the world in which we live contributes to the

---

[4] Ibid.

[5] Dr. No... Francisco Scaramanga ("The man with the golden gun" played with malevolent ease by Christopher Lee)...Goldfinger – did you know his first name was "Auric"? Bond: "Do you expect me to talk?" Goldy: "No, Mr. Bond, I expect you to die." (Of course the means of execution was ridiculously elaborate – a laser beam intended to carve Commander Bond apart like a Christmas goose – and, predictably, JB escaped.)... And, the greatest of all times (played by Max Von Sydow, Christoph Waltz, Telly Savalas – who killed Bond's wife – Charles Grey, and the legendary Donald Pleasence), the Persian cat stroking SPECTRE boss ("Number One"), Ernst Stavro Blofeld.

ever-growing, mammoth prison system in the United States.

And in the government's unending pursuit of efficiency, the growth in incarceration has created an industry unto itself. For our purposes we will call it the "prison services and technology industry" or "Jail-Tech" for short. And it's against this juxtaposition of skid row and Private Equity that Simpel and Associates unexpectedly discovered how a little thing called trust could improve more than just the bottom line.

Levels Man – Avicii (R.I.P.)

Block 1: "It's a dirty job but someone's gotta do it."
- Mike Rowe

For society to function properly, "Jail-Tech" companies must exist.

Yes, it is true that the firms in this industry make money from the prison system, but without them, basic needs for some of society's poorest and most vulnerable families would not be met.

Whether a person deserves to be there or not, prison impacts everyone associated with the incarcerated individual. Without someone taking on the risk of making things work, the imprisoned and their loved ones would become even more isolated and disadvantaged. In turn, society suffers greater harm…and the wheel keeps turning.

Crime is a global problem, and it is well known that when someone goes to prison, the likelihood of them reoffending and returning to jail is extremely high[6]. Think Jean Valjean from Les Mis[7]. It ain't easy on the streets. Believe me, I know.

---

[6] According to an April 2021 report by First Alliance, a non-profit organization committed to improving the financial lives of the formerly incarcerated, 70% of those incarcerated in the U.S. return to prison within five years.

[7] Les Misérables, by Victor Hugo, 1862. Later produced as the "sung-through musical" smash, Les Mis (Claude-Michel Schönberg – music, Alain Boublil, Jean-

Jail-Tech firms provide everything, infrastructure-wise, that enables life in prison to survive. In addition to the prison population, there are also staff members at the facilities, and countless other individuals on the outside who count on this system to function as expected.

From local farmers to the phone company, major industries are involved in the maintenance and operation of this system in a system.

Someone must ensure the plumbing works, the food is prepared, bedding and clothing are available in all sizes – the list is virtually endless.

But today's Jail-Tech companies go farther.

Leveraging modern technologies like IoT[8], these organizations make it possible for people to transform (no more appropriate place to use that word) from "those who are confined away from" into "those who contribute to" society. Modern technology makes it possible to give folks who have "paid their debt[9]" a

---

Marc Natel - original French lyrics, and Herbert Kretzmer - English lyrics. (I'm guessing they chose "sung through musical because no one was going to pay big bucks to attend a French Opera in 1980!)

[8] The Internet of Things (IoT) describes the network of physical objects – "things" – that are embedded with sensors, software, and other technologies for the purpose of connecting and exchanging data with other devices and systems over the internet. These devices range from ordinary household objects to sophisticated industrial tools. With more than 7 billion connected IoT devices today, experts are expecting this number to grow to 10 billion by 2020 and 22 billion by 2025. https://www.oracle.com/internet-of-things/what-is-iot/

chance to live reformed lives while ensuring the dangerous people end up where they belong.

Like any other business with a "guaran-damn-teed[10]" resident population," investors have begun to take notice. Stable contracts combined with incredible opportunities for product expansion and growth has made this once niche industry an attractive location where firms like leading Private Equity investors can park their time and capital. New money means new ideas and growth into areas previously unconsidered. Add a heapin' helpin'[11] of very smart people and you have a powder keg of innovation just waiting for someone to light the fuse.

If this market almost sounds weirdly altruistic, you know, well… it is.

Healthcare is a little similar. It seems odd to make money from someone else's affliction, but without considerable investment, there would be no live-saving drugs or surgical techniques to save you or a loved one.

And who says altruism and capitalism cannot coexist?

---

[9] Danny Ocean (the ever urbane George Clooney): "Now they tell me I paid my debt to society." Tess Ocean (Pretty Woman's own Julia Roberts): "Funny, I never got a check."
[10] Used by many, most notably Dwayne "The Rock" Johnson in 2003 prior to WrestleMania XIX.
[11] From The Ballad of Jed Clampett (The Beverly Hillbillies), composed by Paul Henning, performed by Lester Flatt and Earl Scruggs.

If the collaboration is executed well, people benefit and business is good, what's wrong with that?

Like my grandfather used to say, "If you are looking for stable work, open a mortuary."

Technological innovations are giving people a chance. We live in a world where almost any classroom in the world can be accessed with a handheld device. Education = lower recidivism, which in turn = falling crime rates. Good stuff.

But wait. There's a problem. No one objects when the good people in the hospital take care of Nana after she falls. Nana loves everyone. Nana makes great cookies. Everyone wants Nana to be around a long time. Now imagine the difficulty of being innovative for "the congregation of the damned[12]."

The folks who are "guests of the State," are not Nana. Your client base is not exactly pinning out the trust meter.

Oftentimes, they can be the worst humanity has to offer (for the purposes of argument, we are going to exclude the wrongly convicted). One could argue they do not deserve the products offered by Jail-Tech companies.

---

[12] Title of the fifth studio album by the American metal band Atreyu (Hollywood Records and Roadrunner Records, 2009).

They have done something wrong – they deserve the situation they are in.

So, what happens now when an industry enmeshed in controversy takes on Private Equity capital and now has the responsibility to deliver promised returns? How do you hit the throttle of innovation in a market bubbling with mistrust? How indeed…

The Devil Wears Prada. Directed by David Franke (2006)

Block 2: "You f*&%ed up; you trusted us"[13]

- Eric Stratton

"Trust" is a funny word. We all know what it means, and it always evokes the same emotion. Even in foreign languages, the word radiates power.[14]

In every business, trust plays a central role. Clients trust manufacturers to deliver goods. Providers trust clients to pay for their services and on. Although Frank Ebb and John Kander proclaimed that "Money makes the world go 'round,"[15] nothing starts in business until someone flips the switch labeled "Trust."

I always remind the team here at Simpel that as companies grow, simple, annoying things can quickly become big, costly problems. When we were a one-person shop, I could manage QuickBooks, client delivery, and getting the groceries at the same time. Since we have grown, we employ ongoing financial support to manage our expenses and staff payroll. If I tried to do it myself, it would be impossible. How much more so a competitive, global company!

---

[14] In Hebrew, the word for "trust" is "emes" (pronounced "emet"). It is formed by the first, middle, and last letters of the Hebraic alphabet. The symbolism is unavoidable. For something to be true, it must be so from the beginning to the end.
[15] A song used in Cabaret and sung by Joel Grey who, in at least one person's opinion, stole the award for Best Supporting Actor from Duvall, Pacino, and James Caan (all in The Godfather).

When businesses expand to serious scale, such as when a company exceeds a few hundred million dollars a year of revenues, previous annoyances can escalate past the point of aggravation and become risks that can meaningfully impact day-to-day operations.

If you are in the business of selling cars, you don't want to explain to the board that you missed your sales goals because of a snafu in accounting.

When the good folks in sales close a complex deal, they do so on the assumption that the product will be delivered, and the client will be onboarded and set up for success. This way Sales can get back to selling and getting that next big relationship.

As businesses naturally mature and processes serve more people, they systematize so they can repeat and scale. When this happens in a focused way, the processes experience a shock, like how gravity concentrates matter in a black hole. When this tipping point is reached, best practice often dictates stand up of a central body to navigate the change. This central body is called by many names including IMO, TMO and PMO[16] and will be referenced throughout this book.

---

[16] IMO = Integration Management Office, TMO = Transformation Management Office, PMO = Project Management Office. These are common acronyms for the temporary organizations used in best practice transformation programs. They represent the central location of truth for a project or Center of Excellence. Because they are temporary, we refer to them as Kinetic Work Structures or the work structures that enable the program to channel work energy into meaningful output

Alphabet soup aside, these organization constructs, whether they consist of a team of 12 or one person part time, are responsible for one thing; making sure the project delivers on the goals management wants when it wants them.

As programs scale into organizations in their own rights with their own gravity, these central bodies often morph into the core processes that make daily future work inside a company possible.

This system, working in harmony, or not, is what consultants commonly call the "Target Operating Model".

The "TOM" as it is colloquially known is the personification of how work gets done across functions to keep the lights on and win in the market.

Central business service teams have evolved a lot. What started with Shared Services and Centers of Excellence have become temporary, built-for-purpose digital offices like the IMO mentioned above. And for these teams to be successful they simply cannot waste calories on plumbing. We must all just trust that work will happen in harmony for the good of the project.

---

and outcomes.

Or more simply; the best organizations display the ability to articulate a strategy (or direction), and then turn generalities into meaningful initiatives. Fast. They deliver the work results as planned according to the calendar set with the customer.

Or "What we promised, when we promised it."

As a mentor once said, "I begin every meeting with a recap of 1. what I said I said I would do and 2. then what I did."[17]

Wash…rinse…repeat.

Sounds simple, but if you set the pattern and stick to it, you build trust regardless of the number of people with whom you do business. And yet, why is this so difficult to sustain at scale?

Quite simply the system breaks down because the ideal scenario is a vacuum but the real-world isn't.

There are always external pressures, like noise, coordination across teams or geographies, and more

---

[17] This gentleman helped create one of the largest and most respected financial services/technology companies in the world. He currently serves as CEO of a large, rapidly growing asset and wealth management company. Looks like he knows a thing or two.

separating the world we imagine from what we experience.

It is no wonder our research reveals, time and again, that alignment rather than technical detail, is often the primary cause of program failure.

That's right.

The problem is often not that people can't do it. Or that some science or technical aspect is missing. Rather, most often it is in fact the soft stuff that makes the difference.

Think communications, culture, teaming and more.

Any student of organizational psychology will say "no shit Sherlock"[18] but if we know this, then why do we continue to fail at change?

Year after year.

No matter how much we invest.

Sometimes businesses need to change fast. Other times, the change has been a long time coming. Getting all the

---

[18] Apologies for the crude language but if you lived in Staten Island in the 90's then you are familiar with the Wu-Tang Clan and this gem of a saying. I simply could not resist including it here. Staten Island Strong!

pieces to collaborate and deliver better products and services in-market, sometimes at the same time, is like raking leaves with a drinking straw.[19] Imagine how much more so when no one trusts "Janice in Accounting" or "Simon in IT."

Failure at scale, especially in foundational areas like trust, can literally destroy a business. Especially in a highly regulated industry like the Jail-Tech space where government plays an outsized role. Anything from new regulation to a bad press piece can result in a violent course shift and give day-to-day operations whiplash.[20]

For success to even be remotely possible at this scale you must trust the team or person one desk over to play their role and be there when the ball arrives.

After all, "This is Sparta!"[21]

We call the collaborative machine designed to turn ideas into tangible products or outcomes across any system of trusted actors the "Strategy 'TO' Execution" value chain. This value chain represents a previously misunderstood, critical fail point in many organizations.

---

[19] Many pundits estimate a 70% failure rating. That's like buying a dozen eggs only to find (when you get home in anticipation of out-of-the-oven cookies) that 7 of them are broken. No cookies...unhappy cook.

[20] "Not my tempo!" Okay, a little obtuse, but J.K. Simmons fans will get the reference.

[21] Gerald Butler's battle cry from the movie 300

Not only during times of transformation and immense change but also during day-to-day activities.

In business jargon we term the day-to-day potential problems that could impede our mission as "Risks" and when they manifest "Issues".

Think of Risks as "we don't trust the system to work or deliver as planned or needed." Ensuring Risks are proactively managed, so they don't become Issues that derail the project takes precision. It's like a giant game of telephone with messaging, collaborations and what sometimes feels like cabals acting in concert to deliver what is supposed to be a massive, game-changing outcome.

Trusting this system will work in a big company is like trusting the phone company to get the power back on after a storm. Even when it gets done it always takes too long, lacks transparency, and causes what seems to be a disproportionate amount of frustration on the road to the outcome.

Ensuring that this Strategy 'TO' Execution highway is free from debris like Risks, (e.g., miscommunications) and Issues (funding not available) so the project can be trusted to deliver on its aims is a big part of what experts like Simpel and Associates do every day. It's why Kinetic Transformation and KTA[22] were created. We specialize in quickly creating connections that are built on processes and data our clients trust so we can all get to working together and delivering value sooner. Even across disparate systems.

Kinetic Transformation understands Strategy 'TO' Execution as an interactive governance model that we call the "Kinetic Work Chain." Each step builds on the one before it to produce a virtual rinse and repeat flow of work to test, learn AND execute on ideas all at the same time or as we call it, Act, Learn, Repeat®.

It's kind of like how my mentor approached things. Conceive it, build it, test it, tell people about it, and make sure you do it better next time, all at the same time.

These are all ideas we can understand and appreciate regardless of the product we sell or service we deliver. And that's the point. As Steve Jobs taught us all, when you keep things simple, they tend to work as planned. This allows you to then focus on more important things, like in his case, how the device looks and makes the user feel.

---

[22] Kinetic Transformation is the first universal work algorithm. Kinetic Transformation Accelerator is the first Transformation Management System (TMS). It contains a patented technology called Real-Time-Data-Capture (RTDC). For more information, please contact Transformation Insights, Inc.

These are just basic ideas any modern business should know and yet they always seem to be lacking at one time or another on large projects, like transformation initiatives.

Over more than two decades of studying change, I have found that no change program works without the core concepts I speak of. The more that a program or Center of Excellence[23] travels along a smooth Kinetic Work Lane, the greater the likelihood for success.

It's as simple as that.

After all, it's just not possible to institute a change if you do not take the time to do basic tasks (like conduct discovery). You must research, learn, and study. How else can you proceed with confidence?

Knowing there are governing principles on which any successful transformation project is grounded is a good thing.

---

[23] For those who may be less familiar, a Center of Excellence (CoE) is an organizational construct designed as an internal service provider for a large company. Think of calling an organization's central accounting office. Oftentimes specialty areas, like Tax, may be organized into a central place with standard processes so the complex service can be provided expertly and efficiently. This differs from the oft-confused term "shared service" or "shared services center," which refers more to central places where you can find generalist services. Think: General Administration Pool (Shared Service) vs. a Customer Excellence Team (CoE).

As my earlier book, Kinetic Transformation, argued, if focus is placed on central core ideas with precision the rest seems to "all work out." Obviously, major changes are more complicated, but you get the idea.

The concept is to reduce big scary transformation programs to their basic repeatable components and solve them with uncomplicated techniques that are easy to accept as best practice. We all know what these practices are so why make it more complicated than it needs to be? With the right data flow and basics established early, everyone, from subject matter experts to full time employees, consultants and vendors can interact based on core processes we all know and love.

Over the last four years at Simpel and Associates, we have shown that this approach (followed correctly) greatly increases the likelihood of success at even the largest and most critical change programs and when managing delivery functions dependent upon strategic planning and analytics, like a Center of Excellence.[24] After all, if we trust one another and agree to basic

---

[24] So, what about the times when it's not followed? Simpel is not perfect and there have been times we didn't go the distance. In each case where this happened, we've been able to trace the failure to the base methodology. We've found that when there is deviation from the base methodology that is not being addressed for whatever reason, the change program is likely to fail. Because of this, we're able to identify it and escalate it as a risk so that our clients can make the decision whether the deviation can be addressed constructively or whether they need to end the program before it wastes more money. In this way even when a KTA engagement ends prematurely, we're able to provide the client valuable data that minimizes loss.

ideas, like "large programs need goals and objectives," no matter what goes wrong, or where, we can always trust that we will find our way home: a regulated zone where work is standard, predictable, and valuable. We can always return to the day to day.

When I first introduced this concept at a recent global client, my business partner was initially skeptical. For years the company had been implementing Agile techniques only to be left with a hybrid mish mash that only seems to accomplish one thing: annoying everyone. So why would this more systematized approach work?

The answer: introduce the way of working with a simple to use system that guides by providing basic services and captures data as it is created during the course of work. When pure data is captured like this, it can be structured for use later on in the program when it is needed.[25] But today's technology empowers us to do more than plan and simplify work. If we understand large change programs as requiring integration of previously unrecognized influencers, like Trust, then we can use the system to baseline what good looks like.

---

[25] For example, on day 1 of a project, my first order of business will likely be to understand my stakeholders. Who is on my team, who is impacted and so forth. As the program scales and impacts more people in the organization, that very same data will be useful for performing more sophisticated activities like developing change and communication plans so the masses can learn that new skill or new technology in one shot. If we know these data points will be needed later and in different ways, a system can store that data and make it accessible as part of the process. To see this in action, please schedule a demonstration through info@simpelandasociates.com

We can also create measures to understand how good correlates to the work actually being performed by teams and captured in downstream systems. As these measures improve, we can find what is missing and how to fix it.

Like using barometric pressure to ascertain the weather, we can similarly design programs not to be perfect but rather to provide the data we need to make better judgement calls and take more appropriate corresponding actions sooner. Sometimes the readings tell us "There is an imminent hurricane (e.g., a major issue). Seek shelter and regroup." Other times they say, "watch and wait." Either way, if we all agree to basic ideas, then measuring deviation and devising corresponding action at the most basic level becomes much easier.

But where exactly does this data come from? How is it used, and can it even be relied upon to tell an accurate story during times of rapid upheaval?

Even if we all agree on processes, systems, governance etc., there are still basic concepts like subject matter expertise and data governance that require the human touch.

And that's why at the core of any successful Strategy 'TO' Execution system you will find executives, day to day actors (like programmers), and one of the most vital but misunderstood parts of the trust equation.

Incidentally, they are also the true hero of the story you are reading. I am talking about the person or people dedicated to running the project. The person(s) who organize(s) the data, deliver(s) the report in time when you need it and make(s) sure that everything is working right so when you need to log in and find "whatever," it is there.

Without this person or people doing the air traffic control, all you have is a bunch of work streams or functions struggling to be the best. Instead, wouldn't you rather have a coordinated transformation where people work together for a common goal? Where they are guided by universal data and processes that deliver the goal with a collaborative team that focuses less on administration and more on solving that complex problem?

To answer these questions and deliver a true transformation approach at scale, we must first understand those at the center of large change initiatives. Only this time, instead of focusing on the Transformation Lead[28] as a general role, I want to go deeper and focus on the transformation delivery team or person as a whole – the team or person charged to deliver what is commonly known as a TMO (Transformation Management Office).

Many companies inherently understand concepts like "SteerCo" (Steering Committee) and "OpCo" (Operating Committee), but they don't understand the people involved in executing the day-to-day in the trenches work of a large change project. We believe this is a big reason for current inefficiencies in such a large and diverse market like the global Transformation Industry.

Once we understand who these people are and why they are vital, we can define their roles clearly. And once we align on that, the rest (like the tools) should fall into place.

At least that's how it usually works. :-)

House of Lies, Directed by
Matthew Carnahan (2012)

Block 3: "What exactly would you say you do here?"
- The Bobs, Office Space, 2000

I once quoted the movie Office Space to a client. Yeah, seriously.

I got a great assignment with an international bank to redesign part of their customer acquisition process for large loans. Like mortgages.

The CEO was a lovely and talented woman. She was fun-loving, hard-dancing, shrewd, and tough as nails. She moved with grace but was never hesitant to act aggressively and decisively when needed – everything anyone would want in a CEO. We'll call her Sally.

The kickoff was close at hand, and I got the call.

"Hey Nathan, this is Sally. We're looking forward to seeing you. How's two o'clock to address the entire company?"

Dumbfounded but always eager to please, I said yes. I thanked her for the opportunity and hung up. I buried my face in my hands and yelled. "Oh shiiiiiiiit!"[26]

---

[26] Uttered every few minutes by someone in the corporate world but immortalized by Paul Newman and Robert Redford when they hurled themselves off a cliff in Butch Cassidy and the Sundance Kid. (Redford: "I can't swim." Newman (laughing): "...are you crazy? The fall'll probably kill ya."

When showtime came, I followed my standard routine and arrived half hour early to check out where I would be speaking. The office complex was starkly white and nestled in trees.

After the usual beeps and clicks at the check-in spot, I was ushered into a room that was large – and again, starkly white.

At the front was a stage.

When everyone was settled, I scanned the audience and launched into an impassioned speech about the importance of the program I was there to deliver.

As part of my talk, for some reason I said, "My team and I are not the Bobs. We are not here to damage your work or ask you what it is, exactly you do here because our goal is to work with you to help you do what you do better for your customers and shareholders."

From that moment, whatever the audience may have thought of me, they knew where I stood and what I was there to do and, frankly, not to do. But what helped most was that Sally got up right after me and reiterated what I said and her commitment to follow through on this promise.

Stories like this are very common in the best run projects. It always takes a first mover on the inside to vouch for an idea before it can make headway. It's almost like until you're viewed as a "friend of ours"[27] you cannot begin to take up the mantle of a role and deliver a task collaboratively.

But gaining the leader's support is merely one part of the adventure. Every meeting or interaction becomes yet another story in the books of your brand and also credibility that could easily tumble with a single mistake. Or as my dad likes to say, "It takes so many to create good but often so few to turn it bad".

During times of change the impact can be far greater.

Especially at scale.

As a mentor used to say "the problem with change is that the instant something goes wrong somewhere, the naysayers will point and use that to cause trouble. Then before you know it that little spark becomes a brush fire that can quickly burn out of control."

The best companies understand that large and complex programs are not delivered by a single person but a collection of people with different interests, ways of working, tools, and systems. And this mix becomes even more chaotic when you introduce external parties like a consultant, contractor, or another such service provider. These third parties bring even more entropy to the

---

[27] Donny Brasco (1997, Mike Newell, director)

system as they introduce their history, culture, processes, and ways of working to an already challenging situation.

As ideas travel from Strategy 'TO' Execution in today's work environment they are supported by core work activities that we call the "Kinetic Work Lane". Examples of work activities comprising the Kinetic Work Lane include discovery, project planning, risk/issue identification and escalation, change planning, stakeholder analyses, business case creation and more. The Kinetic Work Lane is necessary for a transformation to be successful.

In today's solutions, these activities are often delivered across disconnected, highly fluid groups of people, communication channels and systems with different data that all need to fit together. With each participant, way of working and system fighting for influence, no wonder organizations waste billions on transformation. It can be like trying to paint the Mona Lisa as described through a game of telephone played by Kindergarteners.

Recognizing this problem, leading companies have turned over delivery and oversight of these foundational elements of large change programs to a new breed of specialist. We refer to these specialists as "Kinsultants" in Kinetic Transformation vernacular.

Kinsultants are super users who live at the intersection of change, process, and technology. As the program's stable, trust officer, their job is to use systems to solve problems and get leaders the information they need to make the hard choices sooner. These professionals live in the slippery and ever-changing world of transformation by choice. They are not bothered by ambiguity because their job is ambiguity. They like the challenge that comes with working in quicksand. They like reinventing themselves and re-emerging every now and again as a better, newer version of themselves for the sole purpose of helping you get your job done.

This new role is about understanding how to use, find and gather the right data and determining how to share it. Kinsultants are solution executioners extraordinaire with a twist; they are also basic system subject matter experts. They know how to stitch disparate data together from different systems quickly and deliver the needed, trusted information when the boss defrosts and asks for it.[28]

Sometimes these folks are called by the misnomers "Project Managers," or "Change Managers." In reality, they are Marines we all trust to push through when the organization needs them the most. They are critical members of the team who make magic happen daily.

---

[28] "I've been frozen for thirty years, okay? Throw me a frickin' bone here. I'm the boss. I need the info!" Michael Myers as Dr. Evil Austin Powers: International Man of Mystery (1997, Directed by Jay Roach)."

Like "The Few, The Proud "[29] the Kinsultant operates with a singular focus:

Create an environment where foundational work happens fluidly so strategy can be realized at a healthy operating pace.

When you think Kinsultant, think "technology-enabled partner" vs. mere concierge or maître de. We are talking about a person who understands the work happening and how to use tools to capture and organize information for later use. These folks can also lead and create the foundational project processes you need when you need them to move a project forward. They are process and way of working agnostic because they use basic, common processes to support the basic, common work every project must complete to succeed. It is their ability to keep it simple and focus on the basics that makes them objective and trusted and by extension, so important.

Data stewardship is another key feature of the Kinsultant's day to day work life. They know how to spot trends and use project processes and tools to prioritize the most important trends and deliver them to decision-makers early so they can make better decisions sooner. Because Kinsultants are objective manager-

---

[29] "The Few. The Proud. The Marines." has been used by the Marine Corps since 1977. See https:// marineparents.com/marinecorps/motto-and-slogans.asp for more details.

producers of foundational work and data, they also run the cadences that focus the multitude of project participants generating the work needed, regardless of way of working, to drive the program or idea forward. They are the ambassadors of kumbaya and their ability to effectively influence change is a key differentiator.

Kinsultants can also organize data into the formats you want or need at the time you want it. Today's tools offer integration and reporting capabilities that Kinsultants use to create consistency and identify options so you can focus on choosing a path and influencing others rather than preparing that presentation for the one millionth time.

As Kinsultants become more experienced and specialized, they can fill more of the day-to-day demands of the Kinetic Work Lane. This includes what is commonly thought of as "change management" or micro level changes like teaching new skills to individuals en masse. Using integrated data at the heart of a program, they can bring consistency and scale to big ideas even as they support team members while delivering technical work, like training, at scale.

Many of the best Kinsultants are even skilled at configuring SaaS products. From maximizing investments in work automation to connecting data in disparate systems that just need to work together[30],

Kinsultants often perform repeated analyses that become the lifeblood of a strategy's forward momentum.

But the technology expertise does not simply reside in pulling the data alone. Today's transformation technology ecosystems also demand integration; something modern API and cloud structures just so happen to make easier than ever.

With the right tools, these business-critical team members provide leaders with on demand data and "solutioning" at the speed of business. Using technology, they move faster across time and space, working so the whole cohort of actors can build the next solution without worrying about things like basic project reporting, which can often be laborious and of limited big picture value.

For a long time, these super users were misunderstood. I found myself in this role on more than one occasion. Anytime I tried to describe my work, people left with a confused look of, "Wow, that sounds complicated, but I have no idea what you just said."

This phenomenon has gotten better over the years as leading consultancies have begun writing extensively on the relatively new standard of a Chief Transformation

---

[30] Common examples include work automation with Agile systems, Human Resource Systems like time tracking and financial forecasting and more.

Officer role and it's supporting department. But there is still more work needed to understand the foundational aspects of a program and the Kinsultants that make them work. What is at stake is not just noise or semantics but the very fabric that makes a project work and a $Trillion+ global industry tick.

When these people are properly understood they become empowered to deliver the data, analytics, and outcomes we all trust. The Kinsultant (often housed in or adjacent to the Office of the Chief Transformation Officer) occupies center stage across all forms of any large-scale change (a.k.a. transformation initiative) and even within the ongoing organization structures.

A system built on trust is a powerful thing. And once you fire it up, it becomes kinda hard to stop. Our research shows a direct correlation between a large change program's success and its efficiency delivering on foundational work, like building trust. We call this collection of work "Kinetic Work Activities" and when they work together in a collective manner, the "Kinetic Work Lane".

When these foundations are solid, trustworthy and manned by someone accountable for objective maintenance, winning at change becomes easier. That's why Kinsultants are not merely project managers, change managers, or operating model designers who save you lots of money (which they do). They are all of the above with the added benefit of using technology to fluidly make the foundational elements of a program or Center of Excellence work.

With this understanding in mind, a picture begins to emerge. And like anything else, a vision of governance, or a system begins to form – not just a technical system, but one that integrates people, change and technology, together into the flow of business. This system becomes a virtual living work database destined to do nothing but get better with time as it is used by experts who know how to improve it.

Change nerds like me understand the potential for this type of system and the analytics it can produce.

For now, let's just agree – it's a big idea.

The Lego Movie, Directed
by Phil Lord &
Christopher Miller (2014)

Block 4: "It's called a shadow P&L"
- V.P., Global Investment Bank

When work central to any finite program is properly organized into its basic components across an interactive value-chain, it can be repeated and digitized, no matter how complex. Especially now that we understand the actors at the center.

Like salespeople before CRM, if we all know what the basics of good process looks like and who the users of this data are, then we can create a system designed specifically for these users during the complicated situations we know as business transformation initiatives.

But before we get carried away, let's remember that just because it is possible to digitize anything these days does not mean it should be[31]. It is easy to get carried away because of the many options, with just as many features that seemingly snap together as easily as Legos.

The good news is that today's best tools make it so easy to create a beta solution for testing and learning. The risks associated with investing in digitizing processes are much smaller than even a few short years ago. Out-

---

[31] "Your scientists were so preoccupied with whether or not they could, they never stopped to think if they should." Jeff Goldblum as Ian Malcolm some time before the velociraptors began eating everyone in Jurassic Park (1993 epic by Steven Spielberg).

of-the-box APIs, advances in Cloud Computing and other standards in the modern digital technology landscape have given users the opportunity to connect systems like containers on a transatlantic tanker moving[32] through the Suez Canal.

Take me for example. About three months ago I had a wild realization: "I am a technology CEO." For the last six years I was more or less an expert consultant. About a year or so ago, I ratcheted up a new corporation to house the technology argued for in this paper. Ironically, I know relatively little about technology and yet here I am, with a new technology available for sale in the market.

Okay, allow me to qualify this a bit.

I have zero formal academic training in computer science or physics.

I know a lot about many technologies, but I am not a technologist. I can't program. I can't write equations. And to be honest, my PowerPoint is not necessarily Big Four worthy.

---

[32] Many people don't realize that today's modern supply chain was built on the back of 4 little locks found universally on shipping containers. This "locking mechanism" on standard containers is what make it possible for those gigantic ships to cross Pacific under the most daunting conditions.

But I dream well. I can imagine and I enjoy helping others do the same.

I learned because my job demanded it and I needed to put food on the table. I taught myself using YouTube, poring through Google search results, and asking lots of dumb questions. I've even learned through Tik Tok.

With today's technologies, you can do it too.

Many employees share the same feelings I experienced when large projects that alter how their company works & behaves are stood up.

For [x] years they were in the business of producing [fill in the blank].

Now they must learn new project management and change management techniques that seem so secondary to the burning client demand on their desk. And yet, without this project their very job and company may not stand a chance. It seems almost impossible to both learn and get up to speed fast enough to contribute in a way that matters during times of upheaval.

Doesn't it?

As a Kinsultant, it is my role to motivate this process by constructing a culture that emphasizes how this in-action type of learning is critical to remaining competitive. It is also my role to design this system sustainably and ensure it adds value long after I am gone.

Best practice suggests that this culture and the outcomes it produces are the purview of a department called the Transformation Management Office (TMO), or Integration Management Office, or Project Management Office, and so on.

This "office" represents the physical embodiment, or personality, of the project and requisite administration as defined by best practice. Unsurprisingly this dedicated person or people focused on a change that could cost millions and potentially wreck a company just seems like a good idea and naturally emerged as the go to approach for solving the problem.

And it worked. Right?

But wait, we still fail 70%+ of the time? Even after investing untold trillions. We still fail!

For years the fear of delivering the change and managing it at the same time often ended up driving decision-making instead of strategy. This led to dedicated, multi-disciplinary teams stood up to address this very valid concern and yet… here we are again. In a world where we still fail 70% of the time!

With the "insanity"[33] caused by the "Tower of Babel effect"[34] at last revealed, we can finally begin to understand and more scientifically react to what was previously thought of as "dark energy" or the negative impacts to work as a result of a negatively charged organization.

Today's technologies make it possible for more of us to participate in the world of idea actualization previously reserved only for coders and the most brilliant among us. It would seem Jobs' vision of a world where we are intertwined with technology was more prescient then even he may have realized.

Today's technologies enable organizations to better understand and capture ingenuity because they stand up sooner and in more integrated fashions. Leaders can use this understanding to develop a finer appreciation of work and how to organize it in all manner of ways. From subject matter expertise to true administration, and now even the work germane and unique to large change events, we can augment today's bloat and inefficient TMO systems with a digital transformation management system that democratizes core data and makes it available so everyone involved can focus on doing their work the best they can instead of worrying about whether a task is defined as "Red, Yellow, or Green"[35].

---

[33] Famously defined by Albert Einstein as doing the same thing over and over and expecting different results."
[34] Since the dawn of time, 2 things have proven true... when we work together as a team our power can be almost unlimited. And yet, it is our very ability to communicate and work together that has prevented us from achieving our goals. It's time to do better.

This is more than a framework or method. It is a scientific system that acts as a one-stop shop for critical operational, cultural, and project management data needed to manage a change. It's a place where this information seamlessly dances with related and vital, but currently siloed data from Finance, HR, Marketing, Sales, etc. It's a place where you can get all the digital process ingredients you need, integrated with the communications you need, integrated with the data you need, sliced & diced however you like right out the box. With this approach, any organization can now respond with agility; even in industries like Jail-Tech where regulatory changes can come at any moment.

Through this system "test and learn" can now morph into Act, Learn, Repeat © or the notion that if we know the intended outcome and what to do to achieve it, then we can jump straight to alignment and execution.

When technology is fluidly integrated into this style of active work, it's funny how quickly "no's" become "yes" and "yeah that seems possible if we work together". All of this is possible in a stable environment where teams can learn, adjust, and address blockers or failures sooner & better because they are guided by an

---

[35] A classic early attempt at defining a single, universal operating language for the progression of risks to issues in an organization. This is often the most common tool used to manage and understand programs and also one of the largest wasters of time. To learn more, contact Simpel and Associates.

objective system with scientific precision and limited human knowledge loss.

This more responsive way of working is made possible by combining data from your experiences with the plentitude of available research on what good process and culture looks like integrated instantly into how you act and move thought to action.

The same is true in a large organism called a company. And when this model is realized in partnership with modern work technologies, you have the makings of something unexpected.

Something new.

A first-of-its-kind virtual transformation office that becomes the engine for focusing a project's work, noise, or what have you into outcomes that you, as the customer, desires.

A certified Kinsultant [36] is like an engineer who understands how to do this in a company at scale. She uses whatever available tools to construct a custom blueprint for this engine that will power a particular

---

[36] There is a 4-step certification process to becoming a Kinsultant. We consider a Kinsultant anyone that has gone through the steps of learning & practicing Kinetic Transformation (the methodology underpinning this approach to change) and consequently can independently use the transformation management system to perform the actions we describe in this book.

program. Their job is to use technology fluidly to generate usable data that drives collaboration and improvements of the system so the riders (leadership) can get to their desired destination (strategy realization).

The Kinsultant is therefore not merely a project manager or change manager.

They are not there to solve the change. Instead, Kinsultants are the Change Process owners. They are accountable for creating an environment that fosters the use of common processes and providing tools that guide leaders, subject matter experts, and other stakeholders as they solve the change for themselves. They solve the project's structure so the organization can focus on what really matters – the project's goals.

At Simpel, we call this universal sandbox or virtual TMO a Rakiyah[37]. And over more than 4-years of research, no matter the program we have encountered, when a properly functioning Rakiyah is established, it is far more likely to succeed than otherwise. Said another way, when enough Kinetic Work Lane infrastructure is established and operating at cruising altitude, you are far more likely to fail sooner, fix the failure and ultimately succeed at scale.

---

[37] The word is loosely based on the Hebrew word from section 1, pasuk 6 of the book of Genesis. Generally translated as a "firmament" or "framework". rom the abyss, order was established by creating a Rakiyah.

Having a Rakiyah with it's own gravitational mass so to speak is a good thing because if it has mass we can measure it (e.g. if it bleeds, we can kill it[38]).

But in business, unlike the universe, the customer is also the owner of the system or if you can measure it, you also have the power to regulate it and on and on until you have a full-systematic representation of a business that can also be used to run the business. Ahh... the wonders of modern technology can even make me wonder if Schrodinger's cat is even relevant anymore in such a system?

Back to practicality... Sally comes in Monday morning. How does this help her?

Well, if we know all of the above physics then like your car's dashboard, we can build possesses to support the necessary gauges to provide more complete and active measures because they are provided in real time, across people, process and technology in a single space. Using this information, a system can help a leader measure and adjust tactics based on an almost atomic understanding of the conversion of kinetic energy into motion/outcome or in this case, work.

A properly constructed Rakiyah will possess the necessary systems and indicators to measure this

---

[38] Predator, Directed by James Cameron (1987)

conversion of energy to outcome and that is exactly what today's solution does.

With this knowledge, the Kinsultant, in the same way a race car driver controls a car, can throttle the team when it is moving towards its goals too slow or brake when a risk is coming around the bend. With the visibility and maneuverability created by a properly functioning Rakiyah, a Kinsultant can provide the guidance leaders need to anticipate, react, and accelerate their change to a victory lap.

That being said, what really makes this approach so enticing is how repeatable it is, beyond transformation events to even the most efficient, day-to-day work across the globe…across departments…across P&Ls (and even languages and geographies).

For the uninitiated, a P&L refers to a "Profit and Loss" statement. It is the most basic measure for the health of a business, product, etc. It reveals how much you made, how much you spent, and how much profit/loss you enjoyed/suffered. As you might imagine, the numbers in this report are perhaps the most vital numbers any business has. And almost nowhere else in the world are P&L numbers more important than at a bank.

Banks are the very embodiment of trust in the macro world.

They simply must get it right. And it is because of this very trust with one of our most vital resources, our money, that banks lie at the center of what makes modern life possible.

Every day we count on knowing our balance is 100,000 and not 10,000 because someone made a mistake while working late at night. These numbers simply cannot be wrong. And getting them right is a hundreds of billions of dollars a year industry spanning finance, accounting and virtually every other department across global, hyper-regulated, organizations.

Early in my career I found myself working as a product manager for what is still one of the largest banks in the world. The product department for my division had just been started and no one was sure exactly what they were supposed to do. However, without fail we all recognized that for the "product" we owned, we were responsible for understanding the profit and loss. The P&L.

During one of our weekly team meetings with our S.V.P., we got a shock. "Well, Finance has finally given us P&Ls. Our role is to manage it."

We all stopped and focused on the numbers on the page. One of the newest product managers on the team was a wonderful man I admire to this day; he was a genius and also one of the youngest V.P.s I have ever met. In a flash Brian, let's call him, says, "Wait, it says here that my product is way unprofitable. Something doesn't make sense. There's a cost here labelled 'corporate' that is crazy high relative to revenue."

The response? "Welcome to the Fortune 500."

Ever the savant, Brian decided to take on city hall by stitching together his own version of his product's P&L without the corporate allocations.

Think about that for a moment. Brian's job was to sell sophisticated analytical solutions as part of a corporate banking solution suite. Instead, he spent his days recreating work that a corporate department was stood up to do!

He labored until he created an awesome solution for understanding not only his own product's profitability but also how finance worked so he could report his numbers better next time. Bravo!

But clients want products. Not spreadsheets. So ultimately when yearend reviews came, Brian had to scrap all this to continue fighting to sell a product he would be chastised for any way because an accounting fluke destroyed his ability to show profitability.

His product ultimately did nothing special under his tenure and he eventually left to pursue other things.

That S.V.P. who handed us the report didn't last either but did go on to build a wonderful career at the bank across the street.

If this sounds like a ridiculous story (an industry that embodies trust, penalizing someone for numbers no one trusted and that he tried to fix), I can tell you I see this exact scenario play out every day in everything from finance transformations to global introductions of cutting-edge technology like VR/AR, Blockchain and AI/ML/Robotics. But what's scariest is how frequently I see this in common, foundational processes like monthly forecasting.

A transformation management system, or Rakiyah helps prevent this very issue by creating an early warning system of sorts through the natural course of work. Or, as the product manager's time was spent pursuing a ridiculous endeavor, Finance leadership would have been alerted because measurable, interconnected goals would be missed. This would have pushed management to ask Finance to fix the issue with a proclamation, discount factor or what have you.

Instead of the silly situation I presented, the product manager would have poured his brilliance into fixing the product while Finance delivered on its accountability in an objective fashion. And on, and on the road of positive the change would have happily gone.

With a Rakiyah, we can better understand the "butterfly effect" of daily decisions in work systems and use this data to help us do better[39].

A Rakiyah makes sure there is the right structure so that good data at scale is available at the ready, whenever and wherever it is needed. The Kinsultant stewards this data as they use it in the trenches with the very delivery personnel that rely on it. Using modern systems, this structure is created naturally, smoothly and in the course of things, so the project always fails forward to an outcome, whether good or bad, sooner.

The idea is to get somewhere and know why & how so everyone can agree on what to do next instead of wasting tons of time and resources on spreadsheets to nowhere. With this data we as a team can naturally identify off track sooner and correct it collaboratively before there is a problem and it inhibits the real needs of the initiative.

If I have learned anything from my wife's constant forays into prison reality T.V. it is that in the scariest place on earth, money is as vital as ever to survival. And it is difficult to survive when even the purchase of noodle soup can lead to trouble and extortion.

---

[39] To be discussed further in Human-Coded-Design, patent pending

Jail-Tech firms navigate this perilous environment and the regulatory systems that created it at the same time to provide solutions to challenges like this and many others like it. However distasteful their existence may be to some, this mission needs to get done. And in a business environment like this, you need the right engineer and tools otherwise you are going nowhere fast. And if the best defense is a good offense, then the sooner you get a Rakiyah up, the better.

But the good news is, these rules not only apply to the scariest places on earth. They also apply anywhere else we find ourselves and face the change force head on.

So, what's next. How do we put this awesome people/process/technology into practice?

Unfortunately this requires a little more research. Or to make the ideal TMO a reality we need to begin with one of the most annoying concepts consultants like me love to throw around yet also dread.

A little term…called Governance.

Wall St., Directed by
Oliver Stone (1987)

Block 5: "Governance, I Friggin' Hate that Word!"
- CEO, Fortune 500 Insurance Company

One of the most confusing aspects of consulting is knowing when it's over. How do you know the time has come to move on from a client or project?

In one respect, you became a consultant or transformation practitioner because you like variability in your work. You probably thrive under pressure and enjoy working across teams, groups, ideas, etc. But like three old fish and guests,[40] projects you once loved may eventually grow stale and it does the soul and psyche good to find another pasture in which to graze.

On the other side, as you get older, stability becomes kind of nice. New avenues for exploration and excellence give you broad exposure and a depth of experience, but settling in sometimes allows you to drive home the point (and the difference) with greater effectiveness.

Still, there is a fine line between continual change and cultural chaos. The best consultants know the difference and when it's time to pack up the cases, they wave goodbye and wish everyone the best.

---

[40] Ben Franklin, he of the electrocuted key and the first fire department, once said, "Guests, like fish, begin to smell after three days." While bathing facilities and the like have significantly improved since the days of chamber pots (ewww), the adage remains accurate in the abstract.

At Simpel, we do engagements in what we call Kinetic Work Cycles. They are discrete 3-to-4-month engagements designed to deliver immediate value but also be easy to step out and hand the reins back to you, the Client, so you can get back to normal.

Sometimes though, clients decide to take another spin through the cycle and other times it just makes sense to use us as a managed service for 1-800-Kinsultingoncall type support. But the point is that it is our responsibility as Kinsultants to constantly assess our value and if we aren't adding it, to move on in a direct and mature fashion.

Today's gig economy market has a way to go in this regard.

Oftentimes, contracts offer consultants no protections at all; a bad situation for both the client and the professional. It minimizes the work a consultant can do and the value they can add.

That's why systems like the one described in this book are long overdue. The system for foundational program work is simply broken. It is maturing but it is not yet working. We should not be competitors to the big consulting firms but complements. A new form of worker who enhances the work you do so you can do it better, faster, and more reliably which leads to happier clients and bigger gigs. It's relationship building 101 from the early days and today's technology makes it happen with great people and processes but only if they live in harmony. And that only comes with governance. Or in this case, governance for the digital era. A model that is not labor or process intensive but one that lives according to basic universal rules that everyone knows and accepts. Nothing complicated, the simple stuff.

Say you decide to keep things light. You are running a major change and decide you only need a leadership group (SteerCo) for escalations and decisions and Work Stream Leads to deliver the collection of projects and tasks that form the basic transformation initiative. Even with that minimal level of governance, when supported by people and technology across time, science says complications will naturally emerge. Even in its most simple form. These formal or informal friction points in relationships operating in tandem to deliver a project, program or initiative are well known but frequently not proactively approached through a lens of leadership. Instead, Transformation Management is often demoted to a change manager who reports and tries to convince others to act.

Why? This makes no sense. If the person is embedded and they see something they are trained to see every day and fix in real time, why not just empower them in a controlled way so the subject matter experts, laborers etc. can just get back to getting work done?

Today's work environment is such a confluence badness and it is such a shame. Because when the system works in harmony, what I call "Organization ESP" begins to emerge.

You know what I mean. It's when teams just seem to instinctively work together and get stuff done, no matter the challenge. Like what Eric Clapton's band did on the song Rollin' & Tumblin on the brilliant unplugged album. When a seasoned band understand each other and gel, magic happens.

When this "magic" is captured, cultivated and harnessed through a team, you can get a bang at scale or what we call "Transformation Arbitrage" or an irrational return from an investment in change.

And ironically like the laugh energy in Monsters, inc., it is far more powerful to get there on a happy, well-built system built on objective data instead of the changing sea of emotions found in today's pre-TMS work environment.

Let me give you a very relevant & recent example.

At Simpel we do a lot of work with leading companies seeking to implement cutting-edge technology like AI into day-to-day processes like accounting. If it sounds simple, then you just don't get it.

Implementing AI is so hard because it's not really AI. Think of it more like advanced pattern recognition on steroids with a computer that starts "learning" from patterns and taking an action that impacts people.

Let's make this more real.

Twenty-five years ago, you went to a bank to get a loan. A good banker had the common sense to offer you a credit card and enter a note against your name in a record on her personal machine.

Today, you can open an account online without talking to anyone.

Based on a quick virtual review of your credit profile, you are offered a credit card in your choice of colors… or sporting your university's logo… or featuring scenes from nature. The scene plays out millions of times every day.

Large companies have similar processes only they are serving internal customers like (the proverbial) Janice from Accounting. And let me tell you about Janice.

Janice's life is a perpetual, active fire drill. Her numbers are vital and can never be wrong. She follows hundreds of formal and informal processes a day to six sigma levels of perfection. Why? Because "failure is not an option."

When you replace Janice, you are not only replacing a process, but you are also replacing a relationship. A trust. A feeling of, "I can call you when I need you and you will get it done because you know I'm a good customer." This relationship is not trivial and it's why AI has been so hard to integrate to date. AI is designed by geniuses who may have never worked in a multi-national accounting department while the users are people who live in the real world and are the very folks who matter the most.

The semblance of rules, both written and unwritten, that overlay the real working world is what consultants refer to as governance. To a Kinsultant though, governance is a critical part of the basic structures we use in our transformational work. It ensures we can trust people on the other side of the equation to do what they are supposed to do. But when that person is replaced by a machine, how does it work?

Back to our client story.

We were working for a leading Fortune 500 product manufacturer that makes stuff you use every day. The people there know you depend on them and do not want to disappoint.

The company wanted to modernize certain accounting processes to drive better data – they wanted to rock Janice's world (without even realizing it) by changing what corporate saw as "only a few" of the processes Janice did every few weeks to an automated system.

As you can imagine, the program had its ups and downs. Previous training and outreach activities to more than 1,000 Janice's had not gone over well. The overabundance of high-quality communications meant to help Janice adapt fell on deaf ears. After all, Janice constantly operated in a world of smoldering fires and the last thing she needed was for something to change while she was flying at 30,000 feet putting them out.

Sadly, every year companies like the one I describe spend millions to help Janice, only to be met with opposition and resistance from the very person or people they are looking to help simply because they do not understand the rules of Janice's world. If they did, they would realize making the change was actually much easier than they made it and could be done sooner.

In my early consulting days, thought leaders often understood the answer as "culture" or the written/unwritten rules for "how we do things around here." We can't really measure it, but we know it's there and can influence it. We can at least try and understand it to design better training or communications that will enable Janice to understand and like Jerry McGuire said" help me, help you."[41]

---

[41] Jerry McGuire (Tom Cruise) at the point of pulling out his hair when talking to Rod

Today, this thinking has evolved to digital approaches for standing up the common governance structures used on large programs every day right out of the box. Indeed, if these are the processes that any good transformation professional probably knows as second nature anyway, then there must be patterns that can be predicted as part of a finite program or project. Even at scale.

In a system where we all know the rules, it just becomes like the Associative Property or "Please excuse my dear Aunt Sally,"[42] – variations of the same formula. Even someone living in a chaotic world like Janice needs only to operate according to them from the get-go – and the rest will naturally fall into place. Where we go from there is limited only by our imaginations.

But again, to achieve all this wonderful idealism, we still need basic governance or else we have something more unknown than chaos – something sinister. And most changes, especially young ones, or flailing ones, can often get lost in the woods instead of becoming the game altering change leadership sought. Life goes on, the organization goes on… until maybe one day it doesn't and you then have much bigger problems.

Tidwell (Cuba Gooding Jr.) who has no hair and somehow won an Oscar by saying, "Show me the money." (Jerry McGuire, 1996, Directed by Cameron Crowe)
[42] PEMDAS; A pneumonic that those who ran away from Math like me have probably forgotten. It was taught during primary math education to help students remember the order to do mathematical operations when solving an equation.

Another way we often think of governance in business is the Project or Program Management Office (PMO) to which I refer so often. Basic governance structures provide generalist management for a program's operation. What began as simple note taking and meeting coordination has grown in a multi-billion-dollar industry dedicated to making projects and programs work better.

When these activities accumulate over time, they become more real. Sometimes the activities include managing a regular meeting cadence and asking people to identify in a job aligned with a specific program in a more formal way. The most effective PMOs are dedicated to a single mission like completing a merger or system implementation. The companies, big or small, with the highest likelihoods for success understand this concept and invest in it as regularly as they invest in accounting or other core operations.

PMOs rely on governance to navigate a complex world. After all, if you live in a world of change, you need to latch onto something or else it just becomes a prison, and no one will succeed.

Sadly, this happens all the time and is why the job of project management is so often cut.

When I sit in the rooms to discuss why the position was eliminated, I more than occasionally realize the decision boils down to no one understanding the person's value.

Or I hear, "We needed to cut costs" and it's easier to cut the project manager than the accounting manager.

Does that make sense? You invested millions in a program but decide to rid yourself of the one individual who has been responsible for ensuring the core operations of your multi-million-dollar program succeeds. You might as well lock the brakes on your business and prepare for the skid into a ditch.

Today's organizations live in a constant balance between these thoughts. When times are good, they invest because they want to and can. When times are bad, they are more selective. Without basic rules, no one wins. And frankly this is probably as good a reason as any that change programs so frequently fail.

Like the systems, people, and technology we have been discussing, modern governance frameworks must be agile to accommodate these real environmental shifts. You can no longer leave it to chance. How else can you react to a "once in a generation pandemic" or "once in a generation financial crisis" and so on that ironically always seems to happen more often than not.

What can happen will and either the thinking modernizes, or you get left behind.[43] This isn't complex.

---

[43] I often tell the story of "Tail Risk Hedging." If you attend one of my lectures and are the first to call this out, I'll buy you a drink.

It's the basics. They always come to get you in the end. And that includes focusing on the wrong one as is often the case when the PMO is let go.

But alas, that's not how the system has worked. Until now.

One place we see the concepts of modern governance truly emerging is in our work with Enterprise Program Management Offices (EPMO).

I write extensively about these corporate functions and how they work – or do not. At their worst, these department are often associated with cranking up the best of intentions to centralize, simplify, and create transparency but then often sadly descend into a morass of bureaucracy and people making work for the sake of delivering work. I have seen these functions devolve in the most unfortunate ways, becoming bloated and delivering dubious value. They become "the police" that folks resist instead of partnering with. And at the end of the day, if a company has only so much money, it will logically ensure the accountant producing the P&L is happy, thereby ensuring the continuation of an essential department. It's common sense. We can deny it all we want, but in truth most businesses believe, "We buy new brakes before we get new tires."

But if we know that, why do we keep doing it the same way? Why bother with elaborate meetings, cadences, and governance structures when most programs need more focus, more partnering on the technical instead of the nonsense like minutes from a meeting?[44]

How can we use this knowledge to do better?

The answer begins with technology and better trained people who live in the system and can deliver measurable excellence. But it also involves an attitude shift in the trenches from Technology = Terminator to Technology = Time. When you approach change the latter way, you can do anything. And at scale, the value more than shows.[45]

When we are called into a situation where a project is bloated and off the rails, we often find the answer lies in a lack of definition around their Kinsultant-equivalent's role or the Kinetic Work Lane activities. We then proceed to provide the tools, get the machine running and exit stage left. Millions saved, products launched, jobs saved or whatever else needs to be done gets done and the world moves on until they need us again.

Wouldn't a system just make this easier?

---

[44] Spoiler alert: No one reads those. Think not? Three lines from the bottom, offer a free fishing lure to the first person who comes into your offer and says, "buffalo."
[45] Simpel and Associates has analyzed three of the leading U.S. banks and estimates each could save in the hundred millions, if not billions, just by making work better through a TMS., Contact us for more details

By using technology to create a dependable system with a dependable person at the center, the rest just seems to fall into place. Nature just seems to work that way once alignment or what we unofficially call governance is reached.

I'm a dummy and even I know that makes sense.

"But by defining all this aren't you adding work and people? Isn't that inefficient and the exact opposite of automation?" Well, yes and no.

"Yes" in the small scale but absolutely "no" at major scale. If a bank, life sciences company, or any other business spends millions or even billions a year on change programs that statistically fail 70% of the time, then adding one person with good tech operating under clear rules seems like a very logical answer to me for tipping the scales in a programs favor. And you know what? It is.[46]

Think about what typically happens on most large efforts.

Initial bang.

----

[46] To learn more about this topic, see my earlier work: Everything you ever wanted to know about the EPMO.

Hiccups start.

Exhaustion sets in.

Move to the next thing.

Again, this is another critical mistake I see every day in today's common transformation approach and it relates back to the very theories that spawned these departments in the first place.

These programs deliver lasting change, so it is illogical to believe that the processes used to achieve success will just go away or "Refreeze" as some earlier organization psychologists suggested. It simply doesn't work like that in real life. And like it or not, these processes and systems are part of your organization now and you can either resist or celebrate and get even more value out of your investment in change.

Here stands a big part of Simpel and Associates' mission. We are technologists who design products so you don't need us every day. You still need consultants and subject matter experts. People will always still need people. Our mission is to simply help them work better together.

We focus on the foundational elements designed to enable everyone to work together cleanly. We use technology, like our own KTA, to implement these basic structures, make them repeatable at scale, and help you deliver value with a partner who collaborates with you in transformation the same way the customer service rep. works with you to resolve the issue with your credit card swipe.

Only our road is the Kinetic Work Lane.

Interstellar, Directed by Christopher Nolan (2014)

And it is digital.

And that's a really good thing.

Block 6: "Sorry, Nathan, I Still Hate That Word!'"
- Now Pissed Global CEO of Fortune 500 Insurance Company

Okay, so the last chapter was a bit technical and probably exciting only to true transformation enthusiasts.

And again, therein lies the problem: it's not the framework but getting people to want to do it that way. Believe me, getting people to care about governance is no fun. And that goes for the consultant and worker alike.

And that's another place the Rakiyah concept helps. Our approach to governance makes it invisible to the everyday project participant. It simply has to be this way because the aim of any change effort should be the change not the administration.

A properly formed Rakiyah supported by technology operates behind the scenes, creating linkages across and throughout work at a meta level that goes well beyond standard project management. When piloted by an expert, like a Kinsultant, the governance is invisible. People work as they are most comfortable within the system rather than defining the work through the system. In this way the system remains controllable and understandable to the people who need to understand it and invisible to the people who don't.

To illustrate this point, let's pick again on one of my favorite modern ways of working; Agile.

As I have written about extensively, what often begins as an exciting, attention-grabbing way of working is often not how most people want to work. Maybe it's great in IT or volume-based Marketing departments. Maybe it even gets strong results at first or when you need it most. But then, like anything else, too much of a good thing quickly turns bad. The work you imagined would improve millions of lives in places you never knew goes sideways not because of the product but the way in which the work itself is conducted.

For example, oftentimes when a company decides to modernize or digitize processes you will hear people start saying things like "It's digital transformation so now we are Agile."

Just because you are implementing a technology does not mean you have to use a tool like Agile indiscriminately. The result is an often fast moving, noisy and aggressive Agile team that clashes with people, teams, and systems around it. This can quickly turn sour, like when a team steamrolls a product at the exact moment it needs time to breathe. Agile in the wrong hands can lead to mass inflexibility ("business arthritis" to coin a phrase) and fail points distinct and unique from the true purpose of the work.

Examples like this are why I frequently refer to Agile as a "tool"[47] instead of a methodology. Yeah, it's a philosophy and way of thinking too but it is designed to drive a focused outcome and in practice often implemented as a hammer, regardless of the collateral damage it causes. And like any other tool, not everyone wants to, or even needs to, know how the tool works. That's for the scrum master, project lead or whatever.

When Agile is not used properly, it can actually become very detrimental. Especially when engaging in broad, cross functional work like developing new technologies.

These programs will always require cross functional expertise, almost always involving finance, operations, HR and IT. Think of the common cross functional team developing today's modern SaaS product. Everyone has a role.

From concept to execution, development often requires input from multiple players viewing the product from their own unique vantage point. The operations person is worried about scale across teams. The technology professional is considering how to integrate the product with other offerings and the customer experience teams are focused on balancing features with look, appeal, and desirability.

---

[47] A tool can be a methodology (think Waterfall etc.), framework (Kanban etc.), or a technology (CRM, RIS, etc.)

Getting all these stakeholders to work together is extremely difficult and a common driver of failure. Trying to resolve that with a hyper aggressive Agile team with daily 8 a.m. scrum meetings sounds good on paper. But rarely works at scale over time in this way. Agile is just not designed that way and nor should it be.

Agile should be Agile.

Sales, should be Sales.

And everyone should still be able to play nicely together because we share the same mission; our jobs depend on it.

This line of thought is one of the cardinal reasons Kinetic Transformation stresses alignment before output. If you can figure out how to get folks working together on the basics, the details invariably fall into place and success skyrockets.

Regardless of way of working, technology being used etc.

These tools are features in the system to be employed at the user's discretion as demanded by the system. Not the other way around. Or the tool should not drive the outcome or in this case failure as is typically the case in today's Agile from center driven cultures.

The best cross functional teams understand this balance and build formal and informal systems to maintain peace through ceremonies concentrated on the most important goal: satisfying the end user. It's a leading reason Agile teams are often constructed with a "Product Owner" or person responsible for owning the requirements and product once it leaves development.

Only wait, there's a problem. If this is the case, isn't the user also the builder, tester, end user and administrator too? The Agile leader's role is much more than it appears at face value. Or as my wife likes to say… "the only people who seem to be successful at fad diets are the people selling the diets". Working in this manner across time, across teams is can quickly turn unpleasant. Especially to creative types. And it is unfair for one work group's decisions and way of working to dictate to others who may find it less so.

On the best Agile teams, the user-centric focus permeates all aspects of work. From writing "user stories" over "business requirements" to iterative test and learn cycles with the customer, Agile excels by aligning teams around an almost obsessive focus on the user to drive the outcome.

But what if the desired outcome is not shared across groups? It would then be like drilling a hole in ceramic and hoping it doesn't break.

This has spawned an industry of Agile trainers, fixers, coaches and more. Seems like a lot of money and work to simplify work… at least it does to me, but what do I know?

Standard Agile governance structures combined with tools like Agile project management software are just such powerful 1 – 2 punches that it is no wonder Agile has taken the world by storm.[48] It is simply so direct and focused, how could you lose!

And yet… when Agile teams interact with more traditional teams, such as during product development efforts, the system seems to quickly deteriorate. Oftentimes so much noise is created reconciling ways of working that projects are often halted because people simply can't figure out what is going on. Like the product manager seeking to explain to her IT partner how she would like the product to launch only to be met with a response like "we deliver features in Agile fashion according to such and such schedule and if you don't like it, I honestly don't care because you are one of umpteen users…" Considering the cost to develop modern technology products, rifts like this between build and commercialization teams are very costly and another leading reason large change programs fail.

---

[48] Popularized in the 2001 Manifesto for Agile Software development, within only a few short years, companies around the world began to adopt Agile tools and techniques. From IT to Marketing, Sales, Product Development and more, it is difficult to find another way of working that has caught on faster than Agile.

As Kinetic Transformation stresses, without alignment you are going nowhere. And in this case, the lack of a standard environment in which all work is normalized is the problem. Not the people or the tool(s). They are all good individually. But unfortunately, they seem to break when we need them most: when we need them to work together.

Transformation Science[49] understands the foundational challenges that emerge when there isn't a harmonious place for these things (workers, ways of working, systems of work) to live in during times of complex change. That's why the solution is so frequently a PMO, TMO, IMO etc. governed by a project plan. There is simply no other way to reconcile work other than with an annoying table with milestones that requires work to update and thousands of hours to explain to people who may not even care. This is a part of the waste modern Transformation Sciences is sworn to fight and prevent.

While transformation departments have also done a great job introducing tools that are easy to use and powerful, they are simply not focused on transformation or the change itself. These tools are focused on their own discrete tasks, like project management, work process automation or creative output at scale. They are designed to address specific tasks or challenges within the project. Not the transformation project itself.

---

[49] We use it to mean the study of the change process from a humanistic, organizational, and technological standpoint.

And its why leaders like the CEO I quoted at the beginning of this chapter get so irritated with consultants. They do not care about our newest tools. They care about the project, the team, the organization etc. The tools we as consultants use... not so much. That's why they hire us and are so often disappointed by the "heavy" management structures and tools we always seem to rely on.

And the use of jargon... like the word GOVERNANCE. No wonder so many of the clients we are sworn to help hate us so much.

We always seem to start off promising transparency and silo busting coordination through a TMO and project plan only to so frequently end up slowing things down because of explaining the rules of the structure or forcing folks to work in ways that are not suited to their normal course of work. In essence, we make it harder for people by creating work on the way to making it easier.

Simpel and Associates uses technology to reconcile this need for governance without getting in the way. It understands that governance is more akin to the wiring that conducts an organization's "electricity." When you plug in your lamp you don't want to always wonder where the electricity comes from. It just works. And any modern structure requires standard (and sometimes specialized) wiring. Otherwise, electric energy does not flow properly.

The same is true for a transformation program, which also releases immense energy. With the right governance, we can harness work energy and focus it in the right direction so folks can bring the light in ways we do not even understand. That's Interstellar[50] level strategy worthy of the ages.

The answer therefore becomes standardizing the stuff we know we need regardless of what work we are doing or how we are doing it. We call that standardization the Kinetic Work Lane or, the virtual highway of work on which ideas travel on their way to becoming the products, projects, mergers etc. that drive business forward every day.

So then… if we have the technology, the people, and understanding, what's stopping us?

If every transformation is a project, then why can't we automate it the same way we've automated project management with work management software or sales relationship management did with CRM?

Why can't we just make a product that any industry, from Jail-Tech to Fortune 500 banks, can benefit from? Why can't we make something everyone can use for

---

[50] Interstellar (2014, Directed by Christopher Nolan) – A crushing personal disappointment. We will save my critique for another time, but for now, props to the team for some of the best, scientifically meaningful special effects of all time and for Anne Hathaway's brilliantly delivered speech about love.

transformations or Centers of Excellence, no matter how big or small?

If we have the technology, then we can rebuild them. We can give them…

Superbad, Directed by Greg Mottola (2007)

Block 7: The Transformation Superstore

…A new technology. A new way of doing things. And considering the alternative, it's about time.

When the systems and processes described in this work come together in a single magic box, it is called a "Transformation Management System" or TMS. [51]

A TMS is designed specifically for change and employs measurements that get smarter as you use them.

To be clear, I am not talking about an all in-one platform. Or just another work automation or digitization tool. Rather, I am talking about a system designed specifically for maintaining alignment across all the people, ways of working and systems engaged in a large change effort or complex delivery organization, like a center of excellence. Only through a systematized approach to managing the intersecting relationships to change at the meta level can you hope to ever maintain

---

[51] Hats off to our first board member, Britt Nichols, for coining the phrase. The TMS term was used by Britt during a conversation on a Friday. I was depressed. I was stuck. I had built this thing. It worked, like really worked, but I just couldn't talk about it. Yeah…right…me, at a loss for words. Like always, we chatted. Well, I steamrolled ideas and Britt listened patiently until I was exhausted. Then, his answer was a simple sentence. "What you are talking about is a TMS, a Transformation Management System." Lightning struck and my life's work fell into place.

alignment across all the work and goings on in today's most complex work and delivery organizations.

A TMS sits between and around project management, change management and all of the other work lying at the core of change. It is therefore not competitive but rather evolutionary and simply too easy to ignore.

The TMS is a guidance system that we all use for how to react when in transformation mode, regardless of where we sit in a business. And now that we know it exists, any company simply has to have it in some form or another to compete in today's digital work world.

Sometimes the TMS manifests in a project manager or change manager's daily work. Other times it is a full-blown Transformation Management Office staffed by multiple people. Either way, there has to be some form of tangible office, digital or otherwise, for people to latch on to during the ambiguity of large change if you hope to direct it.

Today, this is most frequently solved with a mix of people, project plans and other solutions loosely driving work across teams.

A TMS changes all of that. By creating a digital transformation management office that provides a location for normalizing fundamental project work regardless of size, scale or context, a TMS is a first of its kind solution to a problem as ancient as time itself.

This new world is piloted by specialists whose sole mission is to help you move your strategy from point a to point b as efficiently and effectively as possible. Across people, process and technology.

But needing something should not equal indentured servitude or long-duration contracts with external teams. Instead, what I'm proposing is a new kind of just-in-time work model supported by people you trust to pilot a system for navigating the choppy waters of change so teams can understand what is happening and like a speedometer, make adjustments to go faster or slower as required.

To be clear, a TMS is not a replacement for a CRM or an automated Project Management System, frameworks, consultants, and methodologies. None of that changes just because you have a central sandbox intertwined with how you work. A transformation management system just provides a place to set up shop, create connections and get the job done. This benefits everyone from the emerging company that can't afford full-time expertise to the programs operating at scale numbering in the billions of dollars. The TMS is like a virtual Transformation Superstore with all the tools and advice you need to get your job done right. Whether you do it yourself or with help, it's "one stop-shopping" where clients, consultants, contractors, and vendors interact to obtain out-of-the-box ingredients for standing up the basics for winning. Where it goes from there is up to them. But at least they know they can keep coming back because whatever they need, it's likely there or can be found by our helpful staff.

Attention shoppers: Special in Aisle 5 – Get 2 Organization Analytics Modules for the price of 1!

In the same place you find the tools for using data in your very own stakeholder analysis project, Jane, our Kinsultant, is available and happy to share a demonstration. She is also armed with automated pricing so check out becomes a snap and you can get to work right away.

And while you are in the store, be sure to check out the C Lounge where leaders can find real-time reports and alerts revealing how their strategy is performing across a legion of programs or companies available anywhere, at any time and on any device. They can also connect with change management experts like me, available to jump right into their data to give them advice in days… not weeks or months.

Yeah. The best part of this Transformation Superstore is the people. The aisles are maintained by both Kinsultants and your employees all synchronously interacting and making your life better. They are all dedicated to delivering the data and information you need when you need it. All the sophisticated tools these transformation dev. ops. personnel use plug right into your data and scale as the enterprise data set grows and needs expand. Combining this with real-time data capture, you get more of that critical mass information you need sooner.

Another really cool feature of the superstore is its mobility.

Like a prefabricated house, this out of the box change action zone is designed to stand up anywhere and at any time in any organization. Nd because the superstore contains all of the "plumbing" already integrated out of the box, it is self-contained and ready for deployment on the customer's terms.

To maintain such flexibility means it must be built on a foundation of repeatable, universally accessible code.

It simply has to be because if it wasn't, there would be training and uptime which would interfere with the natural flow of work.

The masses would naturally reject this which would notify the system and force correction to the specific case.

This is known today as testing and "customization" or "configuration" of a system and are natural tasks part of any large technology deployment.

And as you might imagine, it is when these very activities are done that many programs frequently break down and fail.

But good news, the superstore helps prevent all of this.

Because the technology is designed to fit in and quickly establish a Rakiyah behind enemy lines, it quickly adds measurable value to the transformation whenever and wherever it is introduced[52].

This is a huge step forward over today's solutions because it means many common information security practices are not relevant to the superstore because everything is already done behind a company's own firewall through its people simply working in a systematized way however they already work. Or as we would say… digging in their own backyard.

At the superstore you can even find contracts for offshore work on-demand driven by your organization's actual needs predicted in advance based on your project plan and the work to be done already priced and ready for presentation.

---

[52] I initially wrote pages explaining this and then realized this was the basis for what will hopefully be my next patent.

That's why you now take calls from vendors. Your data is tells you what you need and vendors are simply there to satisfy your need if you want it satisfied.

This means a better sale experience and a better relationship built on a strong foundation of trust from which to grow.

And even if that does not work out. Not to worry. The superstore also sells warranties and ongoing maintenance contracts including out of the box management of the entire vendor selection, RFP and contracting processes that work neatly with any purchasing or procurement center.

You always have a super squad of licensed Kinsultants ready to step in when you need them and disappear when you don't.

Kinsultants are all franchise owned and require certification. They specialize in every known transformation program known to humanity and use the best "been there – done that" systems to support them all backed by the power of the market.

And if trust is at the bedrock of our superstore system, it should be pretty easy to integrate even with other superstores because, after all, we are just looking for products. Whether the product is data from an ERP, HRIS, CRM, automated PMO or whatever, if all the data represents the same organization, we should have no problem managing it, accessing it where appropriate, and using it in new and flexible ways. This happens today and our experts specialize in providing value and, more importantly, showing you how to do it yourself.

If this sounds ridiculous, consider the following.

The other day I got a call from a Jail-tech client I hadn't spoken to in months. He was stressed. The CFO was presenting to the company's private equity owner and wanted to use the TMS Simpel built for his organization to produce the report. Our client desperately wanted to oblige the CFO, because in the world of SaaS, it's not every day a product has "Tickle Me Elmo" appeal.

But there was a problem. Critical data was missing. It was absent because the CFO had not wanted to participate during the stand-up effort. He just "didn't see the value" and now regretted his mistake. For months the system was a hit and driving value at the enterprise level and he wanted in.

We scheduled a meeting for later in the day. But then something unexpected happened. Between hanging up the phone and the meeting, my client's in-house Kinsultant solved the issue, and everything was great.

Instead of discussing his problem we discussed family, careers, the organization and how Simpel could fit in. We thanked each other for the time, promised to stay in touch and went back to our days.

Think about it. There was no data. I hadn't been there in months. Oh, and I forgot to mention, the information was highly technical, meaning it couldn't simply be recreated from thin air. It was historical program data required to drive and manage day-to-day business.

Technology is vital in instances like this but often most lacking. You have all the stuff you pre-programmed, but what about the exception that you missed?

Just because an expert designs the perfect process does not make it perfect. As it has been written: "What can happen does" and it is a future-of-work product's ability to remain useful in scenarios like this where we separate wheat from chaff. The issue it not that you need it, but that the business demands something never anticipated by the designer. E.g. the system has to learn and adapt.

How did my client solve "The Mystery of the Missing Data"? He called his trained Kinsultant, Jack who knew how to use the system governance to reconstruct the data using weekly progress reports and other data incidentally related to the program. He used tricks like triangulating messages based on dates logged in places like Outlook and other disparate systems and whalla! You have more data than you knew you needed. There was apparently so much integration and data sharing in such a friendly system that it bled to others and helped create a picture even when the data wasn't there. The system helped him do it because it and he got better the more they worked together.

That's cool.

"Jack," the Kinsultant, had spent years working as a marketing manager for Fortune 500s. He desperately wanted to do something different, so he migrated to the high-tech world of Jail-Tech. He was passionate about the mission. And the company felt the same way about Jack's career. They trusted each other and both wanted the best but something wasn't working. Jack's career had stalled and the flame of his enthusiasm was flickering.

But then something happened... the company did the right thing. Instead of marking Jack as another failed investment in management or Jack quitting to pursue other interests, the company invested in Jack by putting him on a digital transformation project. The mandate was to build a new custom TMS with automation and integration across their CRM, Agile, and HR systems and processes. What began as a digital innovation funnel, morphed into a modern Enterprise Program Management Office supporting enterprise-wide Strategy 'TO' Execution activities.

The program's success became a full-time role and now Jack provides analytics to senior executives and board members including private equity owners.

These projects are special… unique… vital… and brilliant. And this time, Jack played a leading role. No one had called (until this moment) because Jack had become just too good to need us.

When the full impact of the phone call hit me, I could tell I had "something in both my eyes."

Sure, I was happy because we had a satisfied customer, but I was also hit with a glorious revelation: The very people at the center began to adapt the system and how they used it in a unique manner not originally envisioned by the inventor. Like the i-store, the market took on a life of it's own operating in a universal sandbox stood up with available technologies as varied as email, chat, ERP, HRIS, PMO, Agile and more. I realized what we had here was truly emerging as a science. And that made me very glad.

And it functioned across the most disparate and disconnected departments in one of the most complicated industries I have seen as intended.

And it did it without me.

Jack achieved his dream of becoming part of a meaningful digital transformation team supporting a client who rose to become a senior leader in his own right.

As my rabbi would say, "Now that's points!"

Breaking Bad, Directed by Vince Gilligan (2008 – 2013)

Block 8: "You built a bong out of a gas mask?"
- *Anonymous college student, in the '90s*

As a teenager, young Moshe Gampel had it rough. As a "Brown boy from the Bronx" he knew one thing: how to be afraid.

And it took nearly forty years for him to learn how to fight back.

In the early days of breakdancing and bodegas in the hoods of New York City lived large and diverse populations. Like today, NYC's true beauty can be found in a countless diversity of people living in relative harmony. But of particular interest to the young me was the immigrant population because while my mother is as American as apple pie, my dad's origins are a bit more mysterious.

My paternal grandmother grew up in Shanghai, China, in the flames of the Revolution. Ultimately like so many others, she found her way to America alone, and after years of who knows what, made it to one of the greatest, and largest, cities in the world: New York. An ex-pat from a middle eastern country living in China, you can say she knew what it meant to be different from the very start.

To what I am sure was the shock of the entire congregation, my grandfather, a lawyer trained at N.Y.U., who was from Poland and as white as the driven snow, fell in love with the Sephardic immigrant from China. In an instant, my destiny as an outsider was forged and I can proudly say, with the birth of our beautiful third child, our Sephardic genetics show no sign of fading any time soon.

You could say I grew up in the hood. I know what it is to wake up to the awful ticking of legions of roaches gnawing away inside your walls or crawling across your face. I hated it, but I was never ashamed. I was not "taught" to be proud of my differences because they weren't "weird" even though some kids thought otherwise. They were what made me special. And I loved that about me.

Until I became a teenager.

I admire my parents and the sacrifice they made to give us a life with a white picket fence but believe me when I say, it wasn't easy for me either. Everywhere I looked, beauty was defined as "something other." I had no idea where I fit or if I could. I knew I didn't share the struggle of my Black friends, but I also realized I did not possess the "right" traits emphasized by the cultural propaganda of the day.[53]

---

[53] Don't believe me? Pick up any movie from the '80s or earlier. The lack of diversity is stark. Imagine being five years old and realizing you don't look the way you are "supposed" to look.

As the years went on, and I set out on my life, I had to do something different. I always felt like I didn't fit in, and I was always very depressed and anxious about that. To escape my angst, I often left home and pursued friendships that got me in trouble.

Let me be clear. Like all kids, I regret the stupid shit I did, but that's life. We make mistakes. Sometimes we are punished and sometimes we aren't. Hopefully, instead of being stuck, we will move on – either way that's football.

Every year the Jewish calendar contains "high holidays." During these events, as a people, we believe we are closest to God. Depending on how you look at it, the times are really scary or super invigorating. Maybe you are excited for your five minutes with the Boss because you have a winning presentation.

On the other hand, maybe the guy in charge has "a hankering for some spankering"[54] and you are walking in with just the reason he needs to unload.

Regardless, we all recognize our unworthiness because there is no hiding from the One who is All-Knowing.[55]

---

[54] The wit and wisdom of Homer Simpson.

[55] "But the Lord God said to the man, 'Where are you?'" (Genesis, Chapter 3)

To combat the impossibility of this situation where even the most confident know they will fail, we hold to the concept called "penance." I do not profess to be a theological whizbang, but I am sure all the rabbis, priests, pastors, and imams would agree – without penance we would all be out of luck.

I view my childhood the same way.

It sucked. It was hard. I made mistakes. I suffered for them. But my story did not end with my screw ups. We all know that America is the land of opportunity (our "Michael Jordan" of national mottos). But we should also at least recognize the "Scottie Pippen" – most of us get another chance.

With luck, love, and personal drive, I made it out and reinvented myself as Nathan. Someone new but with the same values because without remembering and learning it would be like investing 90k a year for a college only to leave saying you learned nothing.

When businesses transform for growth, such as when they launch a new product, one of the most important questions you can ask, especially in a large company, is what the cannibalization effect will be.

Like when Apple launched the i-Phone. I am sure someone asked the question "why if a customer has the option between a phone designed to store music, make calls and go online would anyone want something less… like an i-Pod that only does one of those functions?"

Sometimes this is fine and the market is large enough for all to play in. Or maybe like Apple obviously saw, you see the transformation to come, and you opt to embrace the change rather than resist it. Either way, "new" can often mean bad for something or someone else and the best companies need to understand how to manage this. Especially when undergoing what could be a business altering change.

When I first began talking about transformation, experts had a difficult time understanding the difference between the Project Manager and the Transformation Leader. Both are vital on very large programs but sometimes not. Each is important and must work together as part of a system that helps a program or initiative or project deliver on its mission.

But just because you are a Jack of all trades[56] does not qualify you as an expert in a specific field. Sometimes, like an app, it is just good to have specialization and focus in a particular area that is worthy of the investment.

---

[56] "Where did that come from?" – another round. The phrase stems from 17th Century England. While today it is often mean to be positive, its original intent was the opposite. The expression was meant to point out a commoner who did lots of things, but maybe none of them well enough to become a "master" and take on an apprentice.

Other times generalization is just what's needed because, the features by themselves offer too little value for the effort to produce the desired outcome.

It is when these ideas work in harmony that a tipping point of course is reached and you have something that is simply to obvious to ignore. Or when the team eventually accepted that carrying a phone, a pager, and an electronic – or paper – calendar[57] would never match a single, more elegant solution.

The appearance of the multifunction iPhone is a representation of how what we call "Transformation Arbitrage," or the irrational return you can get from change when it's done right can be realized through the proper integration of tools like data, digital processes, and analytical work in a frictionless manner so the user (the leader) can create sweet harmonious music.

Comparing this to today's scale approach is like comparing my abilities on the violin to an actual player.[58]

My professional life only clicked when I began to balance my personal background with the day-to-day work and experiences in which I found myself. When I

---

[57] The Palm Pilot, cutting edge technology for a hot minute, was discontinued in 2011.

[58] A little-known fact about me, I have taught myself 4 instruments and progressively forgot each one. My daughter, Rebecca is the real genius. Yet another reason she is my special... ▢

learned to respect my roots and bring them to the table as part of my work, my product improved immeasurably. My ideas worked better because people understood me and I understood them.

It's a better way to live – and a dynamite way to deliver work.

Believe me.[59]

When companies find ways to collaborate like this, even something like cannibalization becomes valuable. The event may push those in the impacted departments to become more competitive and refuse to go down without a fight. The change may be the precise push they needed to get out of their comfort zones and dust off their old skills – or to develop new ones in an especially important area of focus.

On the other hand, sometimes you might see Gavin Belson[60] and decide it is easier to go with the new way of doing things. Either way, everyone brings their own background to the table whenever they labor together, regardless of the project or work to be done. So, like anything else Kinetic Transformation, we can either

---

[59] I can't find the exact quotation, but somewhere in Private Parts, Howard Stern (played ironically enough by Howard Stern) says something like, "It was only after I started to be myself that my career took off." (1997, Directed by Betty Thomas of Hill Street Blues fame)

[60] Primary antagonist in HBO's Silicon Valley. (Played by Matt Ross.)

allow this energy that is a feature of transformation work to become noise, or we can harness it.

The law of conservation of energy is as relevant for cultural data as it is for project management data like those found in today's leading systems used by virtually every organization under the sun.

The TMS makes real-time data capture of qualitative and quantitative data sets possible and useful scientifically in tandem because it focuses directly on the support of objective strategic aims agreed to at the onset of a large program or Center of Excellence.

Here we arrive at one of the great comedies of today's Transformation industry.

It is so different and yet so the same every time. We all seem to know this and are still powerless to change our fate of 70% failure.

Why should that be? We should demand more. And now we can and actually expect a better outcome.

Now that we understand large change as distinct and known as Transformation, we can use the very modern tools that today always seem to fail because of adoption or data issues to deliver their intended value.

By using a TMS to supply the data needed to power today's SaaS environment, we in turn can build more agile ecosystems that incorporate focused data, properly captured and algorithmically aligned with outcomes and people so better decisions can be made to minimize the impact of failure and refocus outcomes towards what we really want… realization of our strategic goals.

This alignment and drive of transformation work in a focused lane built for a single-minded program or work group is a big part of what makes the TMS so powerful with such high adoption rates. It is forged in battle and when all is said and done, everyone lives with the process because it emerged naturally as an outcome rather than driver of work.

As business professionals, do you really want to fail because a PMO failed to provide enough data at the right time to react?

If I fail, I want it to be because my idea stank or I messed up, not because of some benign process that I don't even want to deal with.

The application for such a real time data capture system for use in any transformational event can be virtually unlimited.

Someone like my wife, a registered dietitian, could use this type of data capture technology when helping patients transform how they live their lives. Imagine the power you could have with a real time capture of personality metrics during a therapy session integrated into predetermined outcomes like "reduce my BMI" or help me "fight cancer" in the hands of specialist, medical experts?

Throw in AI at a data critical mass quickly achieved by doing nothing more than what you are already doing, and you have the new datasets today's system require to help you understand and make better choices.

It's as simple as that.

Even agricultural and manufacturing businesses could use this type of technology in new and innovative ways to improve how different groups come together or evolve – and it would be dramatic.

Let's consider the ever-evolving marijuana industry. Here you have an ancient product, saddled by restrictions, suddenly set free. And I mean very free, at least here in a great many states.

Expanding state legalization and wide-spread acceptance of weed have brought on a burgeoning marijuana market. Some see it as a good thing – others believe it points to the deterioration of society. Regardless, as a business professional, I spot something I don't like.

As kids we all knew what THC was. It's the stuff that "gets you high, dude" but did you know there are multiple variations like THCA, THCV, and more? Each has its own qualities and with today's modern technologies, they can each be isolated to their root properties for exploitation in patients that can't take the same medications as everyone else.

Think about all the commercials you see for "XYZ" drug. The last 5-10 seconds zips through a list of disclaimers and side effects that sounds like a whispering auctioneer. The drug companies want to shield themselves from liability, of course. A happy consequence is also found in keeping people safe. Medications can be amazing miracles, but in the wrong hands, or ingested by the wrong person, they can prove deadly.

Some people can have a paradoxical reaction to medications. Benadryl knocks me out for the day but I know some people who take a pill and run around the house like a hummingbird trying to catch a speeding Ferrari. When not prescribed by a trained and licensed physician or used according to the directions even Tylenol becomes deadly.[61]

Certain behavioral medications designed to help people can make the symptoms more severe in others bringing

---

[61] Scary fact, Tyllenol kills

on horrible side effects like paranoia, schizophrenic episodes and even suicide. I know more than a few people who have experienced this including a friend from work who almost lost his career at a major bank because of it.

Research shows that some people can find relief from anxiety and other behavioral issues through the controlled use of marijuana. It's a game changer for people like this who have previously been in the shadows and had to turn to back alleys for their medication.

So, if the companies manufacturing…ah…growing the product can be the same regardless of a medicinal or recreational designation, how do you differentiate? In some states (mine), the government steps in by reducing the cost for medicinal use and limiting only the best and most potent products to users with a script.

But wait, that makes no sense.

It means regulation will result in people using more of a substance that is still largely inhaled. One can argue that this method allows the government to stay ahead of potential abuse. But some patients report that they feel a little like they have been registered for the Mutant Registration Act.[62] And in my opinion, no matter what

---

[62] Proposed to Congress by Senator Robert Kelly (in X-Men), the MRS advocates

anyone says, I have personally seen lots of people become addicted to weed, smoking many times a day and running up huge habits.

In my state, medicinal users get preferred treatment at the point of sale – faster, more direct service. But so what! So you get in and out sooner. Putting aside the impact to others waiting in line for recreational use, getting in and out of the dispensary quicker than the guy behind you doesn't amount to enough of a difference to value. It just feels off, as if medicinal users are really recreational users who simply had the forethought to get a script.

There are arguments for and against relaxation of weed. Some good comes out of it…as well as some bad behavior.[63] Like the process for getting in and out faster also requires patients scan their state cards like people living in a QZ from the Last of Us.[64] Yea, freedom!

Let's see how it goes in a few years when the political winds change and someone in the government knows all

---

identifying all mutants in an official census, which also documents their numbers, abilities, and whereabouts circa 2003.

[63] I have friends and clients in the psilocybin and medicinal and recreational spaces. They are wonderful, dedicated, brilliant scientists who truly want to help people. I hate seeing their work tarnished by bad behavior and bad regulation. Enough of the moral high ground, back to the story...

[64] An action-adventure game developed by Naughty Dog and published by Sony Computer Entertainment (2013).

about who is using what and their associated mental conditions. And we are afraid of Google. Hah!

When change happens at scale, these types of questions, issues, and what professionals call "unintended consequences" are the natural outcome. Uncertainty means anything can and will happen and the squeeze the new recreational market is placing on a medicinal market just establishing its identity is as serious as any modern, global industry I can think of. So how do you prepare for this? How can you hope to manage the endless exceptions of everyday life?

The answer, of course, is you don't.

The best Change leaders don't try and control whatever happens. Rather they work to empower teams by providing environments where change can thrive.

If Newton's laws are true, then large change should mean large energy. And if the atomic era has taught us anything, it is to always respect the power of the small.

And that's why a system like the TMS is not only good… it is necessary. It helps us "handle with care" so we can unleash the power of change in a focused way that enhances rather than destroys teams.

And now that you know this, how could you ever do this another way?

Medical marijuana patients don't want to lose their rights – neither do weekend users – but unless dispensaries, producers, and regulators work together for the good of the patient, it's hard to see the medicinal weed industry developing significantly in the years to come. If I can get the same product without the hassle of registration and prescriptions, why would I wade through all the bureaucracy? Medical ganga will have to be much…much…much cheaper or it will disappear in a puff of skunky smoke.

When companies understand the culture of the change as the change occurs, it can pick up on ideas it never imagined and better innovate to meet the more current demand of the customer in the digital age.

The people I discuss throughout this work are of course fictional and stylized.[65] Still, the lessons are unquestionably genuine. I share them because you cannot understand change if you have not lived it. This is especially true when the change is personality-defining like a transformational shift in a business. Seriously, how can I help teach transformation if I don't deliver it in the same way it was experienced?

As a transformation specialist I see all kinds of projects, people and systems.

---

[65] "Ladies and gentlemen, the story you are about to hear/see is true. The names have been changed to protect the innocent." (Opening line of Dragnet.) 65 There was a time when the 8-track tape player was "cutting edge."

I study them and do my best to learn as much as I can so I can serve my/our customers better. For a Transformation Superstore to be effective, it cannot lose cultural elements in the name of efficiency. If it is just another platform or place for tools to compete for prominence, it will share a similar fate to all the outmoded ideas that preceded it.

The TMS only succeeds because it is designed to fit into work specific scenarios called "transformation initiatives" or in the day-to-day activities of Centers of Excellence. It is built to understand culture because culture is an inevitable part of any program. As such, if we use an algorithmic approach, we should be able to predict and plan for it – at least most of the time just like anything else.

Again, this is where the Kinsultant comes in.

Like the narrator in my stories, the Kinsultant occupies center stage in a world of tumult and interprets events while keeping the pieces moving in the right direction, so you end up with an i-Phone instead of the Palm Pilot. Sometimes he messes up.

We all do. If we didn't, there wouldn't be the 70% rule and a need for this work. Thankfully, there is also penance or the idea that by using data, we can learn and do better next time. The TMS provides the safe sandbox for this to happen and all participants and impacted individuals participating in the change benefit from that.

The Kinsultant's ability to emerge from the ashes[66] and fight again on behalf of the family (or in this case the program) to accomplish the project or department's goals are what makes him an indispensable part of the team. The Kinsultant's role is singular and primary: the program's success. It's been true for all time.

And companies that know when and how to invest in this core infrastructure by providing the Kinsultant with the right tools are the ones who become leaner, more agile, and better suited to react to change.

These are good investments in whatever market they appear. Good companies know it.

And now, you do too.

---

[66] The business equivalent of the Phoenix, the bird of legend that lived 500 years, set its nest ablaze, and then was reborn from the ashes.

The G.O.A.T, Lionel Messi

Block 9: "The Beauty of Soccer...uh... Futbol."
                - Embarrassed dads in America everywhere

Soccer is an extremely vibrant sport in New York City, especially in the Bronx.

Didn't used to be that way.

The one and only sport back in the day was baseball. And the only sports franchise with the right to exist was The New York Yankees. Any other sports related activity served as slight amusement until Spring Training rolled around.

But the years passed and waves of immigrant families moved in. The Old Guard died or left (like my family) and tastes in music, food...and sports...changed.

Like when I was a kid, I don't remember seeing a soccer field. Now, it seems like I notice them all the time. Funny how your life changes through the lens of parenthood.

We even have a pro soccer team in New Jersey: The Red Bulls[67].

---

[67] There is also another, local team but we hate them as any good fan in any city with multiple teams would. You love your team and despise the other. Kinda like that other, minor league/professional baseball team in Queens somewhere...

I first began to appreciate soccer when I met my wife. Her family came to the States from South Africa in search of a better life away from the horrors of apartheid. Like many immigrants, my wife's family clings to tradition.

The hierarchy is: parents…family…religion…sports. When my sister-inlaw got married, I met my wife's uncle of blessed memory at the same time I was introduced to rugby.

I'd never even suspected a rugby match. I was sure I was watching two teams engaging in a semi-organized fist fight but after a while, I even found myself screaming and cheering for the home team (the Spring Boks).

Sports continue to impact us. Even in ancient times, you find relics of sports. We all know about the Romans and their games. "Are you not entertained. Is that not why you are here?"[68]

How about the Mayans. Ever heard of Pok-a-Tok? Legend claims they used a head for the ball, which is

---

[68] Russell Crowe as "The Spaniard" (Maximus) screaming at the crowd in Gladiator (2000, Directed by Ridley Scott). I have to say it. The movie is pretty good – as such things go – and Crowe did a commendable job, but I have two questions. 1) Why do all ancient Romans have a British accent? 2) Was R.C.'s performance, which won the Oscar for Best Actor, really better than the one Tom Hanks delivered in Cast Away? I mean, really, Tom's primary co-star was a frickin' volleyball for cryin' out loud. "Wilson!"

not true. But in more serious games, the losers were decapitated and their heads were displayed on the court.[69]

Almost since the beginning of time, people have gathered for competition and camaraderie. As I, Robot[70] made clear, there is a natural order for beings to gather together until one steps up and leads to the new normal. The tendency/desire is hardwired into our DNA.

In Nature, most animals form communities. Planets are formed when mass builds and gravity increases. Why shouldn't sports accomplish the same aim?

Given my love of sports, you can imagine my joy when my little son finally expressed interest in pursuing one.

I came home one night and overheard a classic discussion.

Son: "Mommy, did you find out about the soccer?"

Mom: "Yes."

Son: "Then sign me up mom – sign me up!"

---

[69] And the Duke-North Carolina people think they have a serious rivalry.

[70] A film adaptation of Isaac Asimov's story starring a pre-Oscar-banned Will Smith (2004, Directed by Alex Proyas).

Not a word about times, rules, anything. Just, "Sign me up."

Mom was on it – end of story. A few weeks later, our boy was running concentric circles around the soccer ball – without making any move to touch it. And he was having a blast.

Years passed and our little guy has become a strong young man still pursuing his love of the game. He may be small, but he is mighty.

Height is unimportant in soccer. Completely meaningless. Besides, great athletes have always overcome obstacles and defied the odds: Muggsy Bogues[71], John Fosbury[72], Roger Bannister[73] – the list never ends.

---

[71] Paraphrasing Helena (Act 3, scene ii, A Midsummer Night's Dream): "Oh when she's angry, she is keen and shrewd/She was a vixen when she went to school./And though she be but little, she is fierce." 6 Lionel Messi, my son's favorite player, is 5′7″ in a league of players averaging 5′11″. My son would argue, Messi is the greatest ever and it's not even a competition. Size means nothing. Never forget that. 5′3″ point guard who had a 14 year career in the NBA despite being 16.5″ shorter than the average player in the league.

[72] Little better than average high jumper who revolutionized the sport by perfecting "The Fosbury Flop," where he went over the bar backwards. He won the gold medal in high jump at the 1968 Mexico City Olympics. I wax eloquent about this brilliant competitor in Kinetic Transformation.

[73] Despite warnings that the human heart might explode from exertion, Bannister became the first man to run a sub-4-minute mile on a cinder track in 1954.

As weekends turned to years, the little boy spiraling around a ball transformed into a strong and talented player. He's even made a competitive travel team or two along the way.

Watching my son is always fun, but I also gained an appreciation for the game. And, though I am a little embarrassed to admit it, I eventually realized the importance of the goalie.

I knew a goalie had to be quick and lithe, but I underestimated the requisite intensity. He knew where the ball was at all times. He was crouched like a tiger preparing to pounce. He reacted to every move any offensive player made. He could read his teammate's defensive efforts – and recognize the smallest miscalculation.

And he needed to be good, because the defense on my son's team had more holes than a moth-eaten cardigan.

Most of the time, "Lucas" made a stop. Which was great.

Until I noticed a pattern.

Call it a flaw or what you will but I noticed a problem in his game.

Every time he thwarted the opposition, he picked up the ball and boomed a punt down the pitch. The other team recovered it and the assault recommenced.

Eventually, his React -> Stop -> Punt technique wore him out. The constant bombardment of scoring attempts eventually proved too great. And when a ball finally slipped past his fatigued legs and arms, the spirits on my son's team sagged.

Since my son is a striker (offensive position), he is often downfield looking to score. But how can you score when you never touch the ball? Despite his excellence, Lucas forgot a basic fundamental: You cannot score if you do not have the ball.

The gifted young man needed to learn how to pass the ball to his teammates.

Teams, sports and businesses alike, face a similar dilemma all the time.

It's one of the many reasons scaling a technology across an organization can be so hard.

Even when we all want to do it and we all understand why we need to do it, we can't – at least not as consistently as prescribed in the procedure.

Like take one of the great ironies I see every day. The problem of "winning too much".

Everyone wants to win. Especially in business. But when one person has too much success (winning too often) jealousy rears its ugly green head and mistrust can abound.

There's that "trust" word again.

Transformation Initiatives are often mistakenly thought of as "long-duration programs" when we should think of them of bodies of work. Otherwise the change is too big and will be too difficult to integrate at scale.

If our research has demonstrated anything, it shows the need to focus first on alignment and then change. Getting people to communicate and agree to why they are there in the first place is often more difficult than the technical aspects of the program.

And this is true even when cutting edge technologies like VR, AR, AI, ML etc. are involved.

That's why the secret to success and avoiding some of the costliest mistakes a change effort can make begins with getting people to talk to one another and agree.

Yes, we all ascribe to "Go big or go home,"[74] but we still need to Act, Learn, Repeat® or else you never "matriculate down the field"[75].

And that's where the Kinsultant comes in. Bridging the technology with human worlds to guide actions and help the team drive to success on the field of battle. Or in the case of business, in the daily activities the company performs in the furtherance of its mission. Again, the Transformation Superstore comes to the rescue. Like an athletes cleats, it is built for just this situation and has options designed to tailor how it is used based on whatever situation is encountered.

The TMS is just such a technology in the world of Transformation.

The same way it would be illogical to play soccer without shoes, it is now similarly illogical to lead a large change program without a TMS.

We have a "Shaq-attack" esque[76] solution that any of us can lace on and use on the court.

---

[74] The phrase is attributed to a 1990's motorcycle shop in California that was pushing oversized Harley Davidson pipes.

[75] "Just keep matriculating the ball down the field, boys." Hank Stram, Hall of Fame Coach of the Kansas City Chiefs. While more than a few of the players might not have understood the encouragement, matriculate they did in a 23-7 whuppin' of the highly favored Minnesota Vikings on January 11, 1970, in Super

[76] Like all kids, I was mesmerized by his size and dominance. The only professional player for whom free 75 Ahh Shaquille O'Neal, the GOAT at Center of my

But even more valuable than the empowerment of the Kinsultant is the impact such a system would have on helping the rest of us become more proactive and impactful in our own actions.

Pre-TMS we lost this type of "intangible" data in the ether or as noise because work was not appropriately designed to capture it because frankly, we never knew it existed. We just called it "work" or admin when in fact it was the essential oils exerted by any program.

Contrast that with the Kinsultant who is skilled and properly armed to capture and steward this data. Where stewardship in this context is defined as ownership of:

- Preservation
- Accuracy and
- Availability…

…for valuable use by a business partner

The last item, as you might imagine, is the most difficult to define and measure.

How do you define usefulness and value? And is it even worth defining?

---

generation. I'll never forget the first time I saw him. throws just didn't seem to matter, Shaq is one of the best of all time and a personal favorite.

The Kinsultant helps figure that type of question out in real-time while delivering the program and maintaining the balance in the system at the data and process levels the same ways the best Marines care for their gear. Today's methodology-driven approaches are not designed to address these challenges and therefore often do not work this way.

For the uninitiated, it is not uncommon to find in a large corporation a system with:

1. System users
2. System/Solution Owners
3. Product Owners

Knowledge Owners

And more!

All to maintain a single system.

If the mechanic uses a tool, shouldn't she be the one to own it?

Full stop.

And yet, where transformation tools are involved, why then is this more often than not the case?

It would seem to me that systems designed to connect groups potentially operating in a silo would do better than that.

And yet, this is how many businesses around the world operate every day.

What a waste!

Here's a prime example of how this plays out.

Value capture.

What is "value capture"?

If I have learned anything over the last several months bringing a new technology to market, it is that until the customer easily ascribes value, they will not pay attention.

And rightly so.

But this goes deeper into buying psychology. And is why a distinction always seems to emerge between the "sales person" and the "closer". The former works the prospect and the closer makes it rain.

Two completely, interrelated, interdependent roles and skillsets that when forced to work together, always seem challenged.

There are systems out there dedicated to capturing the value from a merger the "right way." Okay…lovely, but where does this data go? How is it used? No one really knows. We just know we need to capture it but how exactly does it help us deliver the bottom line return the investor is demanding?

Ok, so there are project management systems that do this too. But then what? Once the program is done where does all this knowledge go? Does it just disappear and whoever is left has to deal with it?

Often yes.

Deal teams and expensive consultants and contractors move on and the company is left with low cost options that must eek out results that seem to always get harder to fulfill. Businesses are rarely left with these tools once the dust settles on a deal because after all… how else can you charge for people when the work has been automated?

Or how about how the data gets into the system in the first place?

Take a business case for example.

When large companies decide whether to invest in a new technology (or just about anything), someone somewhere makes the case with numbers and facts to convince the powers that be to loosen the purse strings.

If every business boils down to a P&L, surely we should be able to automate that aspect as part of a business case module in a larger system. Right?

Well, yes. But that's the easy part.

The hard part is where and how that business case is used? How is it socialized so that when you get in the room you have already won and are not pitching cold?

Again, these are all standard activities previously thought of as executed by people with high EQ and degrees when, in fact, they are just common-sense activities present in any program orchestrated through disparate, disconnected systems and people.

But wait, if these are common sense, then why do we waste so much time on getting them done?

Again, that's where the Kinsultant comes in. He takes the system out of the box and customizes it differently based on the culture and uniqueness of the organization and situation in which he finds himself. He then uses the system like a speedometer to understand and guide work so the system at the core of all this change remains consistent regardless of the state of change. Or the system the Kinsultant establishes during the change is flexible enough to also grow into a mature, fully functioning business as usual system. And if need be, pass off to more industrial options, like Project Management Technologies.

Only, by staying behind the scenes, in the mix, the TMS ensures as these new SaaS systems and their features are stood up, they never become disconnected or siloed.

No matter how large an organization or work effort grows.

If you ever heard a consultant talking about specializing in "value capture" that's great because that's what you want them to do. Focus on identifying, realizing and capturing value not the processes to get there. A system alone simply can't replace the person doing the action because at the end of the day, it is still people who need to pay the bill and buy into the value. But when a system provides the process, the salespeople and closers can focus where they need to.

Similarly, with the transformation superhighway on which the Transformation Superstore represents. By owning the maintenance of the entire superstore, the Kinsultant sets the players up to perform, or to score the goal, or to deliver the report, or to win the sale, or whatever. Think of Kinsultant's and their daily use of a TMS as being the regulators of the stadium on which the team plays.

Its always advantageous to have home court advantage in sports. A TMS makes this analogy a real possibility at scale. Even during the largest organized change events.

And believe me when I tell you, when business flows like this, you have a much better shot of coming home with the Golden Boot instead of a kick in the pants.

The Big Short, Directed by Adam McKay (2016)

Block 10: "If they are being a pain, box 'em in"
- Managing Director, Global Investment Bank

One of the hardest moments in my job is when I see my client failing.

It makes me feel bad about my work and my contribution for sure.

But what makes me feel worse is imagining how the person who hired me must feel!

When something does not work it is easy to start the blame game. And I am mature enough to realize that there are times when I am there for no other reason than to take the heat.

Sometimes, teams are not breaking through and someone needs to bear the brunt of the frustration, anger, and fear. It's a fact of life, one, unfortunately, that I experienced on more than one occasion during the tenure of my practice.

But the other day I was really upset.

I was working with a client on a particularly gnarly transformation of very manual, rote finance processes. We do a lot of this work because, like I said, the small things can and often will crush a company. Nowhere is this truer than in finance.

Tactical and strategic communications plans to the rescue.

The client and his team were doing everything to make the stakeholders happy but nothing seemed to work.

Not enough training?

Hundreds of pages delivered.

Not enough communication?

Tactical and strategic communications plans to the rescue.

But no matter what, the future users of the client's dream solution were not biting. They were resisting and there was no ambiguity. They were not participating.

As the conversation with the client wore on, I started to ask about the users. Why would they want to use the system and such.

Like any good leader, the client had answers at the ready.

"It will reduce noise and waste in their day-to-day jobs, which they will appreciate," he said.

I dug deeper. "Who are these people?" "Where do they sit?"

As we went deeper, the reason for the resistance became clear. The future users were part of a Center of Excellence (CoE) set up to provide concierge processing and reporting for the business. My client was in corporate and represented central leadership's vision for reducing costs through process simplification. Because – isn't that a great thing?

Well, if you are the people in the CoE, you probably don't think automating a core part of why you are here as "good".

Even if the thing you are automating makes sense, if Maslow[77] has taught us anything, oxygen (or in this case employment) comes first and so people will resist like their lives depend on it. No matter what.

But it was more than just survival in this case. The Center of Excellence was set up specifically to prevent what my client was trying to do: a corporate

---

[77] Abraham Maslow 1908-1970), American psychologist, who formulated the hierarchy of needs to explain human emotions.

infringement on the business' sovereign rights to self-serve their finances, their way.

So yes, AI would save millions, potentially, but how much would it lose because it would isolate people from core financial processes and the people providing them?

Whether you are a transformational lead or not, I am sure this story resonates.

We are conditioned to follow our patterns of behavior and resist change. Maybe I am trying to get healthy for the millionth time. Or maybe it's my son trying to change his dribbling technique. Either way, when we are in the "event horizon" of daily work and life, what we consultants call "business as usual" these types of pattern changes become even more difficult.

That's why a common refrain I use with clients is to make a recommendation "while the walls are open". The idea is, during times of change, people and organizations are a lot more open to suggestion. They need to behave differently. It is their very purpose on the program. So it is often a good time to fix the process or customize that system because adoption will be easier, cheaper and faster.

When things are going according [78] to plan the desire for change is at its lowest and is why the earliest, most seminal theories about change management always begin with "unfreezing a population."[79]

Getting people in the mindset where they are open and receptive to change is a major part of the problem and again one that has been frequently overlooked and misunderstood to the practitioner's detriment.

When someone feels safe, say in a job, the last thing they want is change. Because they are naturally conditioned to avoid it but also because of other things, you may not see. Like maybe this person we are thrusting change upon has a sick child? Or maybe the economy is crashing and someone who felt safe deep in an operational role out of the limelight now faces scrutiny. This can really mess up someone's day and we as consultants sadly often overlook this in the rush to deliver results.

Again, this is where the TMS fits in. It ensures these basic ideas are considered and efficiently delivered relative to their importance to the effort so you can limit these feelings and gain receptivity sooner. Receptivity or "adoption" as we call it in the industry is a major issue in of itself let alone achieving the gold standard of

---

[78] Insert footnote with speech at the end of the Dark Night where Joker explains that when things "go according to plan no one worries"

[79] As always, respect to Kurt Lewin, the inventor of modern Change theory and his seminal work, Lewin K (1947a) Frontiers in group dynamics: Concept, method and reality in social science; equilibrium and social change. Human Relations 1(1): 5–41

success… Activation. Or the notion that the customer of an effort is in fact using the outcome in a measurable way that while it might be related to the change effort, is now independent.

Once you have that, your program can do anything. And frankly you should no longer need a lot of what has traditionally been called PMO to sustain it.

Instead, a TMS enables a more holistic focus or approach utilizing all of the tools at a person's or team's or organization's disposal to its fullest.

That biting point or junction where the meta level (Transformation) meets the focused level (change management) is a critical world we don't even begin to understand today at scale. But a TMS makes it possible to at least begin to approximate it. And that in itself is enough. Or as Sergeant Hartman from Kubrick's masterpiece Full Metal Jacket put it "Private Joker is silly and he's ignorant, but he's got guts, and guts is enough in my beloved corps."[80]

But what do you do when the situation truly sucks?

As the mentor I quote at the start of this chapter used to say "sometimes you just can't put lipstick on a pig".

---

[80] This topic will be further explored in the third and final installment in this series, Human-Coded-Design, coming soon…

Like situations where you need the people who will be laid off to help you deliver the very project you are there to drive?

These kinds of situations are extremely difficult, highly prone to failure and require the utmost care. But there is good news. And unsurprisingly the answer comes once again from the very people we so often rely on. Only this time we have a built-in crew ready to help.

A Change Agent network that stands up with the precision of a firefighting team and the data of the matrix. This crew is led by the Kinsultant and his ability to jump right in with data at the ready to firefight is a big part of the everyday value he brings when he walks in Monday morning.

But like anything in life, not all Kinsultants are at the same level on day 1. And like any other career path, there is a lot to learn and levels to achieve on the road from eager helper to trusted advisor who is accountable for delivering your project on their own. Not dissimilar to my own life journey. And the different grades within the Kinsultant population is how you, as the user experiencing the system understand it. Or in my case I understand it as stages of life and by understanding my stage and resources I can better my odds for achieving my goals.

The same is true for any company and change effort.

Like anything involving people, we are all different.

Even if we can agree to basic rules for how a program runs, we each bring our own backgrounds and cultures to the table as I have explained at length in the previous pages. Despite these differences, be they technical tools (I like Excel, you like Sheets) or cultural (I like Agile, you hate Agile), we still have to work together to get the job done. Failure is not an option and can never be when the mission is so vital.

As the person at the center of the program working on behalf of the team delivering the program, the Kinsultant uses data to tailor the change program with precision. Because the tools are all the same (a Stakeholder Analysis is set up the same everywhere) and we already have data from all over in the TMS, instead of wasting time doing the analysis, the Kinsultant is running reports and interpreting from the start. Adding value in the same visible way others on the team who have been there longer are. And it's understood.

To help a client get to this point requires practice because like all things, the more practice the better[81] you become. And thus, the higher your level.

---

[81] See Malcolm Gladwell's brilliant Outliers.

In Kinetic Transformation, we have a system for this based on our Act, Learn, Repeat way of working. I won't share it here for confidentiality reasons and future works, but suffice it to say it, like everything else we do, there's nothing shocking. A leveling system with clear guidelines for moving up.

But more importantly is asking the why? Why will this be adopted when so many others have tried?

The answer: it already exists in nature so to speak. We are just naming it and bottling it in the Transformation Superstore. It exists because as my dad said when I asked him why the plane would not fall out of the air during my first flight... "because science says so. Now shut up and get ta bed!".

This system exists because it has to. The current system of building and rebuilding common accelerators in separate locations simply no longer makes any sense. The inefficiency is too great and too well understood to continue. Leading companies already know this and are investing in transformation departments the same way they are investing in leading customer service areas in response.

These groups are often flooded with resumes from the top talent because they recognize the likelihood for exposure during change is simply greater than during "normal times".

Top performers crave CEO focus because everyone understands how they fit in and are unafraid to simply do their job in the superstore structure.

With transparency you can do anything. I have seen it happen many times and you **can** do it too.

If you are thinking that this sounds like a high functioning meritocracy, then you would be right. And that's a good thing because in business you should be able to understand your value and why your contribution matters. Or else, what's the point?

Sometimes the enemy during large and disruptive events is irrational. As Alfred famously says in The

Dark Knight, "Some people just want to burn it all to the ground."[82][83] In business where competition and personal survival are at stake, this is never more accurate.

To win today, we need a better, more objective system – there is simply no longer any way around that fact.

---

[82] Christopher Nolan, director. 2008. Alfred was played by Britain's own living legend, Michael Caine.
Did you know Alfred's last name was Pennyworth? (Not to be confused with "Rich Uncle Pennybags" of
Monopoly fame.)
[83] Aragorn is played by a hirsute Viggo Mortensen. I make multiple reference to LOTR in honor of my Dad and my middle son. The biggest and best fans I know!

Like I said to my client struggling with the CoE, sometimes the only way to meet your foe is to meet them on the field of battle. Consider Aragorn's challenge in Peter Jackson's The Two Towers, "Ride out and meet them!"[84]

Sometimes you have to fight back. And when the time comes, in the immortal words of Tony D'Amato, "It's the guy whose willing to die for that inch that wins."[85]

But just because you have to fight does not mean the method by which you battle is determined. Or as Bruce Lee put it… "Be like water my friends."

The Kinsultant, as she grows in her career specializing in transformation, will learn to get better at stewarding data, recognizing trends, and driving them in partnership across groups.

Because the Kinsultant is empowered by the strategy and a transparent system, she lives outside of the culture and can solve complex issues in concert with folks like my clients. And this partnership can prove priceless.

---

[84] Pacino – Game of Inches – Just another in his catalogue of classics: "You're out of order. You're out of order! The whole trial is out of order!" (And Justice For All) "Just when I thought I was out...they pull me back in." (The Godfather, Part III)"Attica...Attica!" (Dog Day Afternoon) and...of course, "Say hello to my little friend!" (Scarface)

[85] The original Lee quotation is: "Empty your mind, be formless. Shapeless, like water. If you put water into a cup, it becomes the cup."

Especially given that many advisors often force clients to ride out on a charger[86] and confront "the dragons" with a sword when it turns out the big lizardy thing is toting a howitzer.

I knew what it was to be scared as a kid. It was reality in a poor, transient area like my neighborhood in New York in the '80s and I carried the fear with me in my early career. I was scared to push (even when I should have) early in my career because I didn't understand how to make my point without driving everyone nuts.

It took me years of work and collaboration to learn what feedback really means vs. what was said and how to help a client see it too.

There is perhaps no more vital aspect to the Kinsultant than the people element. I have worked on programs where companies, properly investing in this aspect not only saved millions in program delivery costs almost immediately but also used it like an i-Store to stand up other, more permanent solutions to other issues across even the most complex organizations. Much like the EPMOs I write so much about. These departments often make work possible at large companies and tried and true models scaled from the fires of Transformation and loaded with the sickest, best indexed data you can find

---

[86] A horse, not the big, weird other plate underneath the dinner plate that you find at fancy dinner parties.

and that gets better the more it is used is something no company will be able to live without in today's digital market. Our research shows it, our clients know it and now you do too.

Remember what Gordon Gecko said. "The most valuable commodity I know of is information."[87] Next time you head out onto the battlefield to meet an impossible situation, be sure to take it with you and you may find yourself the hero in your company's story of change.

---

[87] Wall Street (1987, directed by Oliver Stone)

Austin Powers, The Spy Who Shagged Me, Directed by Jay Roach (1997)

Epilogue: "But what does it all mean, Basil?"[88]

- Austin Powers, The Spy Who Shagged Me

One question remains. "How can I trust the data?"

Implied in the preceding six-word question are the following:

How can I trust that the data will be there when I need it?

How can I trust someone will enter the data so it is up to date?

How can I trust the data is telling me the right message?

How can I trust that everyone else believes the same things?

And on, and on.

Trust (or lack thereof): one of the root causes for transformation program failure. If we all trusted

---

[88] From Austin Powers: The Spy Who Shagged Me, 1999, directed by Jay Roach. (A pale imitation of the original, Austin Powers: International Man of Mystery (1997, also a Jay Roach work) – except "Mini Me" was a nice addition. But no Elizabeth Hurley? Come on, man!

everything to be where it should be, we would all get along and everything would be hunky dory.[89]

But knock, knock. Reality check. The world does not work this way – especially during times of immense, gravitational shifting change such as when your life is turned upside down by a stupid mistake or your company makes the wrong bet. Failure is simply a part of life and you can either learn to work with it or struggle against it like Sisyphus.[90]

A TMS works as your ally and will show you where the stepping stones are, so you have a better likelihood of ending up on the right side of the 70% challenge.

When I first started talking to experts about the concept for what would become my patent application and product known as KTA, the first TMS, the most common question I could not answer was, "So, I come in Monday morning. I turn my computer on, I go to your website, and I do what?"[91]

---

[89] "You should stick around 'cause later we're gonna make s'mores and sing kumbaya." Nicolas Cage as Memphis Raines in Gone in 60 Seconds (directed by Dominic Sena). Did you remember Angelina Jolie is in the movie? I didn't but I remember the name of the "unicorn" car (1971 Mustang Sportsroof) was "Eleanor." Shows you where my mind is now.

[90] Condemned by the ancient gods to roll a boulder uphill only to have it roll to the bottom just before he reaches the crest.

[91] Credited to the current Chief Operating Officer of Transformation Insights, Jason Engelhardt. There's a funny story about this but I'll leave it to him to tell you.

Like any good consultant adept at sales, I tried every answer in the book.

"Reporting!"

Nope. The client already had reporting (and what does that mean anyway).

"Okay, how about workflow!"

Bzzzzzzt! Wrong again. There are a million workflow tools out there. Most don't work as promised and adoption is terrible. Also technology guidelines have become stricter. For practical security reasons, it is hard to integrate data with external providers and unless you've created the greatest tool since Moses' staff[92], you won't sell the client on another workflow automation software package.

Just like that. Every punch I threw was blocked until I had nothing left. One situation was particularly embarrassing.

After years of developing the TMS and the science behind it, I finally started to get attention. I got invitations to places and was "in the room." (Think Shark Tank without the cameras.)

---

[92] The walking stick with which he parted the Red Sea. Exodus Chapter 14 for those reading along.

I was in a meeting with people I had admired for years and I was being magnificently ineffective at getting them to buy in. They pretty much told me I had no shot before I had said the first word. No matter what, I couldn't get them to a place where they could get their minds around the concept of the TMS and why this "wrapper" was so vital. They just saw it as more workflow automation and they could do that themselves. And they were right.

When it was over, in my mind I looked like Stallone at the end of every Rocky picture."[93] To be frank, I had done my best, but, in retrospect, I was not ready. I was learning on the go – and in this instance, the "floor model" just didn't cut it.

My attempt was very much like the 2008 Hulk movie. The pieces of my product felt right – much like the excellent cast of the film.[94] But the CGI was not up to par and the movie did not mesh. It crashed the Hulk franchise so significantly that the character reboot (starring Mark Ruffalo) has yet to appear in a solo feature again. I am neither Gene Siskel nor Roger Eber, but I know a stinker when I see one.

Ang Lee is a brilliant director[95] but he made critical, almost juvenile mistakes in his in vain attempt at

---

[93] Only, I didn't feel like shouting, "Yo, Adrian, we did it!"
[94] Edward Norton, Liv Tyler, Tim Roth, the late William Hurt, and Ty Burrell.

blending a unique interpretation of what a movie based on a comic should be with the best available tech. He needlessly and ridiculously flailed about in a juvenile attempt at manufacturing emotion in a way that demeaned the loyal customer. In the process he also grossly distorted the background for, no benefit, of one of the greatest hero's of all time. I hate that movie. And so do millions of others. In my view it should be "stricken from every tablet" Ten Commandments style.[96]

Consequently, Bruce Banner's "You won't like me when I'm angry" alter ego has been relegated to the role of a backup singer in the current Marvel Universe.

I was terrified I was going to share the same fate. I would have made a lot of noise only to fail.

Worst of all, I should have seen the trainwreck coming. I had already been introduced to "Elliot," a well-known investor and tech enthusiast. A week before sailing the ship of my future into the iceberg, he'd been gracious and generous with his time – and brutally honest in his assessment.

---

[95] Although I'd rather have a root canal than sit through Sense and Sensibility ever again.

[96] To my brother and his wonderful family... I knew you would be upset not being mentioned in the acknowledgements. After all, you were one of my earliest and most loyal supporters. Consider this footnote our inside joke and my way of saying thanks for all you do every day. - MNG

"You have something special," he said, "but if you don't go back to the communications drawing board you will never survive due diligence."

Another example from the world of sports.

Nolan Ryan, arguably the greatest pitcher of all time, nearly quit baseball because no one believed in him. Even though he could throw in the high-90s, he had only a passing acquaintance with the strike zone. When he was traded to the California Angels in 1971, he was introduced to Tom Morgan, the first pitching coach he'd ever had. Almost immediately, Morgan spotted a flaw in Ryan's delivery – and the rest is baseball legend.[97]

I had the business equivalent of a world-class heater; my delivery belonged in a church softball league. But until I could "find the plate," no one would care about the TMS.

Like any new technology CEO can relate to, I threw my hands up in the air and screamed.

"Arrgh!"[98]

---

[97] Ryan leads in career strikeouts (5714) by over 1000. He won 300 games and threw seven no hitters. (No one else has more than four.) He threw his seventh when he was 44 years old. (In a crime against humanity, Ryan never won a Cy Young Award, the annual prize given to the best pitchers in both leagues.)

[98] This is a personal reference to a childhood friend who's mother passed away at the time of the writing of this work. My friend's mother was a kind and generous

I composed myself and proceeded to jump on the phone with my team of Kinsultants. But, instead of failure, my whining was met with a barrage of confidence and trust.

"We won't quit."

"Failure is not an option."

"We can fix this. We understand exactly what this means and know how to fix it."

I hung up, took a step back, and realized what we had: a first of its kind system built in an algorithmic way of approaching big change. So, if we are on point, and change is universal, we should be able to pivot. Right?

We bought a new computer and upgraded our technology. We dusted off our artifacts and got to work. We knew what was wrong and were confident we could fix it together. In a matter of days, we completely redefined our model and targeted the next iteration to be ready within a month. Early field tests have been very promising and hopefully in the next Kinetic Transformation milestone I will be talking about the product's success.

---

woman who didn't have a lot but gave as much of her heart as she could. She was kind to me. Took me in when others did not and always made me feel like I mattered. Even if all I wanted to do was play Nintendo and D&D. To my friend in the fortress, here's to the game that should've happened. May you be comforted and only know happiness for many years to come. - MNG

Submitted for your approval: A full reposition of an MVP that I spent my life savings to build, disrupted and rebuilt with a full marketing and sales strategy executed in days - not months. We had the concept, it was the positioning that needed fixing and that, actually turned out to be the easy part. Or at least we hope it is. :)[99]

I am beyond lucky to have found the core teams at both Simpel and Transformation Insights. They are friends and colleagues who provide invaluable support. But beyond the niceties, the concept works at scale across the globe (even out of a basement office) because it is built on common processes and supported by a core technology called a TMS.

This is a real concept that customers have used to generate millions in revenues and savings while bringing disruptive new products to market – products you probably use every day. These clients worked with a single consultant who used an integrated approach to bring a program to life and position the client for success and use of the systems for what has already become years.

Almost everything needs a tune-up now and then. And as we/I make our own transformation from boutique consultancy to what will hopefully one day be a leading

---

[99] Sarcasm of course... communication is the hardest part after all and the very problem at the core of why we are here.

technology company, we never forget to eat our own cooking and always push ourselves to make it better.

That's what teamwork, as a system looks like working in harmony at scale.

That truly is the TMS and what Simpel has stood for since the beginning[100]: making transformation less scary so folks can do what they need to do to win. We provide the road on which you travel to the big game. You don't want to worry about potholes on the road to victory and you similarly don't want to fail because there was a big risk buried in ops that never made it to a place where leadership could actually do something about it before it failed.

Sometimes things aren't as quick changing as a start-up, and you want to go faster. You need someone to guide you through the data, the quick start systems, and the available processes because you want to do some cool stuff without bothering with an investment committee (a.k.a. Discovery).

This is how the modern, flexible organization runs and it only happens with a technology and specialty team at the center. Companies that "get it" operate across the

---

[100] I designed "the girl on the water" logo with Rebecca to convey the message of emerging from rocky waters to a clearing – going through the torrent of transformation and emerging on the other side where you row cleanly and win the race.

globe because they can turn on a dime.[101] The rest are…
Gimbles.[102]

Contemporary enterprises trust the data because the data comes from people who are part of the process operating in a system they trust to deliver a complex change every day. It all just works together because of the system. The scale is the easy part.

Investments in systems and people are never a bad thing when they provide the basic infrastructure on which your team drives change. Whatever solution you have will never be perfect. The motor will always strain under change; sometimes you will need someone to help you get over the hump.[103] And that's when you need a franchise person who can proactively step in, help you get it done and then get out of the way so you can get back to your day. It's how business should work. So why can't it operate this way in the transformation

---

[101] Under the heading of things you don't need but that might help you win Trivia Night at the local pizzeria." Turn on a dime" morphed from the phrase "turn on a five-cent piece." That expression first appeared in 1881 in reference to a well-trained horse. Even though you did not ask, the expression "playing on a dime" (from the 1920s) points to a baseball infielder with extremely limited range.

[102] Long a fixture in NYC (founded in 1842 and expanding to expanding to 53 stores in 1965), Gimbel's shuttered its doors in 1987 after failing to adapt to changes in consumer demand.

[103] I do love origin stories. "Over the hump" springs from the vernacular of American service personnel to describe flying over the Himalayas in the early 1940s as the U.S. ferried supplies to Chiang Kai-shek in China, who was fighting the Japanese.

services market without all the noise? The answer is, it can, it does, and it's awesome.

Organizations that operate within basic work norms, like those described by the Kinetic Work Chain, will lead the evolution from Gig Worker to Transformation Worker and reap the benefits.

Kinsultants represent the new, twenty first century entrepreneur who provide vital operational system and IT support, including subject matter expertise on the very processes on which a program or Center of Excellence runs. While the information may not be central to the change[104] it can very well represent the difference between success and failure. Kinsultants are therefore part of an equation that delivers the trust needed to make the relationships that are critical to change work. So if these people are needed, let's empower them, at last, with the right system to answer the call.

The solution is not a direct workflow but a general sandbox or playground where work can occur with all the fun tools you need to succeed. It's like a cloud for work where process, digital, and people of all kinds meet on clear, unambiguous terms. This one stop global

---

[104] e.g. you are not changing to generate project reports. The information is a feature used to drive your goal, which is an integration, merger, or whatever the change may be.

shop is critical to the future of work and, like Amazon in 1994, its time has arrived.

As I like to say: It's not hard, it's Kinetic Transformation.

When programs and work are reduced to their mathematic basics, running a variety of computations is easy. Processes or actions (the emergency analysis you needed yesterday) can be facilitated with a system that gets you the data you need, integrated with the templates you need along with the communications technology that helps you align leaders, get sign off, and return to what you were doing before that last-minute fire drill disrupted your day.

Technology today in the right hands has the power to do this and make work better for all of us who depend on it every day.

This system exists today. It is being used and there's no telling where it will go next.

Or who it can help.

Imagine if you don't want (or can't afford) a four-year degree but want to participate in the one trillion dollar+ global digital transformation market? I've seen many people, like Jack do just this – so why not you.

For heaven's sakes, look at Dr. Dre!

He started out as a rapper from the hard streets of Compton and became a billionaire (for a time) selling a digital sound product promoted brilliantly via music videos. It wasn't even a great product! Sony was much better. Dre is a genius at marketing and combining forms of media in recognizable ways. If he can do it, you can too.

Long-term contracts often translate into lasting headaches. Entrepreneurial types want a plug and play standard for today's fast-paced work the same way companies do. So why should there be so much friction in contracting, onboarding and offboarding? This transformative way of working is not only ready to emerge; it has emerged and is being used at leading companies today. That's why companies need to standardize where they can now or else they will not be able to take advantage of the gig economy. Because after all, there is always more work in the Transformation Superstore. Work never ends because transformation never ends. And don't you want to win?

Here's the bottom line. Owning change and taking the accountability that comes with it are real, quantifiable things when big change is at stake. Taking on this awesome responsibility should not be done alone. And a universal transformation system helps distribute that risk so the organization has a chance to win. And isn't that what business is all about anyway?

Universal ingredients like common, out of the box toys or Kinetic Nuclei, integrated into a user playground with the simplicity of an Etch-aSketch[105] is the promise today's technology brings. The TMS is merely the vehicle for riding in the Kinetic Work Lane. And the results speak for themselves.

We began with Jail-Tech so let's close there.

I've watched more "Inside the Prison" shows than I care to admit, and I know one thing for sure. In prison, you follow the rules or you have a problem. That's it.

Business, of course is not or should not be prison. But today's competitive digital work world sometimes feels like it and is always looking for a fight. With so many things working against you, is it even possible to win?

The answer, I am proud to say is yes. And companies from the client in the story above to others in industries as complex as Jail-Tech are benefiting from this new way of working.

And it's time you did too.

---

[105] Introduced in 1960 for $2.99 (now about $30), this magnificent invention by André Cassagnes was inducted into The National Toy Hall of Fame (who knew?) in 1998. It has sold over 100,000,000 units.

As Pacino said in his speech in Any Given Sunday, "Either we heal now, as a team. Or we will die as individuals. That's football guys… that's all it is… Now, what are you gonna do?"

Today the TMS and the Kinsultants at the center represent the team ready to follow your lead. It is time businesses truly released the power of change and achieve what I like to call Transformation Arbitrage or the irrational, almost unimaginable returns that come from learning to dance with change.

Sometimes this return is unhappy. And other times… sad.

No one can help that. That's just football.

But with technology working with people as part of a cooperative system to help the team win, then at least what we can control… we probably will. And in turn, be more likely to succeed.

These are truisms of life… physics, mathematics and business.

When we hope, what can happen sometimes does.

And if you don't believe me, ask my buddy who went from being stretched over the front of a police cruiser's hood to twenty+ years of happy marriage, beautiful kids, and more joy than he can list.

Peppermints indeed…

www.ingramcontent.com/pod-product-compliance
Lightning Source LLC
Chambersburg PA
CBHW070423290526
45791CB00005B/1811